Tie it t
Moon

Eddie Kerr

LONG
TOWER

A Long Tower book from
GUILDHALL PRESS

Wherever there is life, there is contradiction, and wherever there is contradiction, the comical is present, and wherever present, therefore, one is justified in ignoring the pain.

Kierkegaard (*Concluding Unscientific Postscript* 1992:513-4)

Humour is the least important thing in the world and yet the most important thing in the world.

Published in May 2003 by
GUILDHALL PRESS
Ráth Mór Centre, Creggan
Derry BT48 0LZ
T: (028) 7136 4413 F: (028) 7137 2949
info@ghpress.com www.ghpress.com

Guildhall Press is a Social Economy enterprise.

Printed by Universities Press, Belfast

© Eddie Kerr / Guildhall Press
All rights reserved

ISBN 0 946451 72 9

Supported by the Arts Council of Northern Ireland.

This project is supported by the European Union, administered by the
Local Strategy Partnership for the Derry City Council Area.

**EU Programme
for Peace and Reconciliation**
in Northern Ireland and the Border Regions of Ireland

**ARTS
COUNCIL**
of Northern Ireland

LOCAL STRATEGY PARTNERSHIP
DERRY CITY COUNCIL AREA

Contents

About The Author

Born in the Creggan Estate of Derry City in the North-West of Ireland, Eddie has been involved in creative writing, broadcasting and drama for the last twenty years and during this time has written fourteen plays and four short films. He has also published short stories, poetry and articles for the stage, television, radio and magazines.

Eddie is a member of the Irish Writers Union and Irish Playwrights Society. He has been Artistic Director of the PlayStation Theatre Company (based in St Columb's Theatre in Derry) for the last seven years.

As a regular contributor to BBC radio and television, he has been involved in many wide-ranging productions, including ideas generation, scripting, programme production, and even performing his own material as a stand up comedian. Recently, he has merged all his artistic skills into a One Man Show which has toured extensively and successfully in the USA.

Two of his plays have been performed on the New York stage: *Packie's Wake* at the Helen Hayes Theatre in March 2000 and *The Guildhall Clock* at the Gromack Performing Arts Centre in October 2001. His plays have also toured Ireland, Scotland, Canada and Spain.

Eddie uses his dramatic expertise to work with people who have a range of social and personal problems. *One in Four* is a drama documentary on mental health, produced in conjunction with STEER. *It's Like This* is a school-based production on bullying and teenage pregnancy which is currently on an all-Ireland tour. The productions are accompanied by interactive workshops for the audiences. He is currently working on a number of new projects.

Eddie is also Assistant Director of the Verbal Arts Centre in Derry, which promotes literature in all its forms and employs fourteen staff with up to fifty artists on its database. Last year, over 26,000 people attended events and programmes at the Centre. The Centre also offers interactive multi-arts programmes for young people aged between six and twenty-six years. Over the last five years, the Artemis Team at the Verbal Arts Centre has worked with almost 10,000 young people, many of whom experience a variety of social and emotional behavioural problems. Eddie uses arts education to help create a safe and conducive environment where pain and hurt can be resolved as part of a healing process.

As an experienced arts facilitator, he offers a wide range of workshops and master classes in drama and creative writing. He has offered these services throughout Ireland and Europe, and, in recent years, has been a regular visitor to the USA to do the same. He has worked extensively in New York, Kentucky, Virginia, Ohio, Tennessee and Oregon. The workshops are based upon the contention that the participants should be given every level of support and professional advice to 'tell their story' in whatever format they feel comfortable with.

Previous Work
Full-Length Plays and Films

Something for Nothing (short)	1982
Beatin' Docket (The Devlins)	1984
A Future Tense (Play and Film)	1985
Yanks, Tanks and Nikki Cakes	1990
Outward Bound	1991
Rites of Passage	1992
The Guildhall Clock	1994
Packie's Wake (The Devlins 2)	1995
Red Hot Lovers	1996
Different Voices	1997
Good Days and Bad Nights	1997
This Is Man Made	1998
The Legends of Samhain	1998
Aileach (A Celtic saga)	1999
One Night Stands	2000
Under Pressure (Play and Film)	2001
The Big Do! (The Devlins 3)	2001
One in Four (Documentary)	2002
It's Like This (Play)	2002
Over the Moon (Musical)	2003

The Verbal Arts Centre

Promoting Literature In All Its Forms

Language is the most powerful tool possessed by mankind. The Verbal Arts Centre aspires to bring together the spoken and written word and to unite listening and reading with speaking and writing. It regards the oral tradition as an important seedbed for written literature as well as for conveying the musicality of language and a sense of community and identity. The Centre stresses the creative and imaginative potential of language and has consistently promoted the right of every person to be able to articulate his or her feelings, dreams, aspirations or fears.

The Centre believes that arts education provides people with opportunities to examine human experiences. It offers participants a powerful mode of expression. It helps develop intellect by expanding the capacity for creative thought, exposition and critical thinking. It offers participants the ability to bridge the real and the imagined, the concrete and the symbolic, the practical and the inspired. Creative and cultural education enables all people to find their own voice and develop the skills to service this. The use of creative activity in any setting allows a broad and narrow focus to be adopted and, at the same time, work towards clear measurable outcomes. Above all, the Verbal Arts Centre provides people with an opportunity to find their own voice and tell their story.

The Verbal Arts Centre employs artistic activity to help people to look, see, do and understand. The arts can help us comprehend, understand, express and communicate our experiences, feelings and ideas. The Centre employs a range of activities that help develop new ways of looking at issues, concepts and problem solving in a dynamic and entertaining way. These activities promote and enhance a wide range of subject areas across the curriculum.

For further information contact: The Verbal Arts Centre, Stable Lane, Bishop Street, Derry, BT48 6PU (028-71-266946) or info@verbalartscentre.co.uk

The Verbal Arts Centre, Derry.

Fourwords Or So...

Youse are probably wundering wae ye bought this buk in the furst plaice, so ill tell ye why if ye houl yer tonge. Ye bought it cause it celebrites twinty years riting by me. I hive bean working (editor's note: to labour, toil, strive, sweat, forage, graft and do the bizz) fur the lass tou dicades slaven o'er a brokin pensil and wile slaggin. Imagin, o'er the lass rake a years I hive ritten furteen plays, a wild rake a sturies and puems an im fed up so hears the ress of the oller stuff wot I wrotten, gallered and stored awae fur a rinny dae. An if ye luk out dae windae, it's rennin.

This is not so much a book as a collection of writings, hearings and voices that I picked up along the way. Some original, some plagiarised, some borrowed, some blue. Some came to me in the depths of despair or in the throes of debauchery, and me being my most cynical about the life we lead. If you heard some before, I'm sorry – if you haven't heard them before, amta wild creative? However, I have learned that there are two great secrets to success in life: the first is to not tell everything you know.

This is dedicated to a long-suffering wife, Annette, also Tara, Shane and Kevin. A posthumous dedication to Me Da, whom I miss a lot, and Me Ma who never missed me in me life, as the marks will tell (only joking, Sheila). I would also like to acknowledge the support of the many family, friends, artists, work colleagues and of course Derry people, past and present, home and abroad. Special mention to Paul, Joe and Declan at Guildhall Press for their welcome advice and professional input.

I want to express sincere thanks to all those who have helped me during my creative career and have shown faith in me and my work. I thank each and every one of you for your time, help and encouragement.

Go raibh míle maith agaibh
Eddie

Poetry

14

Tie It To The Moon

'Tie it to the Moon,' he shouted, as the morphine kicked in,
Sullen, ashen as the boyish charm drained from his face.
Pain is wicked, twisting nice people like Plasticine,
Moulding snarls and grimaces into frightful gazes.
I could end this now but the chemical smack dulls and soothes.
My Da had the voice of a crooner, and he knew it,
So did everyone; Old Blue Eyes Frank knew it, but that's life!
I thought it was corny, even square, man; don't sing that; as my face
got redder, Frank got more jealous, Old Green Eyes.
He was noisy even on his quiet days.
But he was stronger than Atlas, braver than Dan Dare and smarter
than Holmes, My Da.
He could make an empty room laugh and a packed room silent.
Lying there with translucent tubes exploding out of every orifice,
The eyes that once sparkled like fireworks looked as empty as a clown's.
'Tie it to the Moon, son.' I couldn't do that; even Frank couldn't do
that; only My Da could do that.

I Hate Poetry If It Doesn't Rhyme

I hate poetry if it doesn't rhyme.
I hate poetry that has no time-ing.
I hate the stuff that sounds so metaphysical
As the poet tries to be ever so mystical.

I hate the way poets write about love,
The sorrowful soul and a God above.
I hate the lines that have a moral
Or metaphors that sound like coral.

I hate them poets with their moaning dirges
Unburdening their pain with gloating purges.
Above all, I hate the poet's bland sincerity
To see the world with such apt integrity.

Only Shakespeare Could Do That

I would love to write a Shakespeare sonnet,
But how would I know what metre or rhythm to put on it?
Perhaps I could write about the good Lord above,
About the loneliness of despair or my true love.
Or even steal Burns' ode to a red, red rose,
Or Tennyson's sea where the sharp wind blows.
Or Heaney's eulogy to the hobnailed boot,
Or Milligan's heroes wearing sharp Zoot suits.
Or Yeats' analogy that a terrible beauty is born,
Or Shelley bleating on how his love is forlorn.
Or Durcan, MacNeice, Shaw or that ilk,
Telling me, metaphorically, that poetry is like mothers' milk.
How the masters define the world in rhyming couplets,
Odes to passion, that's the fashion, you define it.
How the sonnet can last for sixteen lines,
I'll never know how I'll do mine.

It's An Oxymoron, Baby

I stood at the bar holding my plastic glass, trying to act naturally.
I heard a silent scream, then I saw her.
She was wearing a genuine imitation fur and fake pearls.
She was pretty ugly but looked terribly pleased with herself.
She was standing in a small crowd eating diet ice cream.
She told me she was on a working holiday from Great Britain
Where she was studying political science and business ethics.
She clearly misunderstood my intentions: 'Good grief!' she said.
I felt like one of the living dead, found missing in a government
organisation.
The CD player was playing a new classic, soft-rock number taped in
front of a live audience.
Now and then, I felt alone in a crowd but, like all extinct life, the
lounge lizard has had its day.
'It's an oxymoron, baby;' her response was a definite maybe.
'Sweet sorrow,' I thought, but I didn't really care because by then I was
legally drunk.

The Hand

Last night I held a little hand
So dainty and so neat
I thought my heart would truly burst
So wildly it did beat.

No other hand did I hold so tight
Or could greater gladness bring
Than the hand I held last night
Was four aces and a king.

Did You Know...? (Or, I Wanna Be A Pig)

If you yelled for eight years, seven months and six days, you would have produced enough sound energy to heat one cup of coffee. (*Hardly seems worth it.*)

If you pass wind consistently for six years and nine months, enough gas is produced to create the energy of an atomic bomb. (*Now that's more like it!*)

The human heart creates enough pressure when it pumps out to the body to squirt blood 30 feet. (*Oh, My God!*)

A pig's orgasm lasts 30 minutes. (*In my next life, I want to be a pig.*)

A cockroach will live nine days without its head before it starves to death. (*Creepy...I'm still not over the pig.*)

Banging your head against a wall uses 150 calories an hour. (*Do not try this at home... maybe at work.*)

The male praying mantis cannot copulate while its head is attached to its body. The female initiates sex by ripping the male's head off. (*'Honey, I'm home. What the...?!'*)

The flea can jump 350 times its body length. It's like a human jumping the length of a football field. (*30 minutes... lucky pig... can you imagine??*)

The catfish has over 27,000 taste buds. (*What could be so tasty on the bottom of a pond?*)

Some lions mate over 50 times a day. (*I still want to be a pig in my next life...quality over quantity.*)

Butterflies taste with their feet. (*Something I always wanted to know.*)

The strongest muscle in the body is the tongue. (*Hmmmmmm...*)

Right-handed people live, on average, nine years longer than left-handed. (*If you're ambidextrous, do you split the difference?*)

Elephants are the only animals that cannot jump. (*OK, so that would be a good thing...*)

A cat's urine glows under a black light. (*I wonder who was paid to figure that out?*)

An ostrich's eye is bigger than its brain. (*I know some people like that.*)

Starfish have no brains. (*I know some people like that too.*)

Polar bears are left-handed. (*If they switch, they'll live a lot longer.*)

Humans and dolphins are the only species that have sex for pleasure. (*What about that pig??*)

It Was Love At First Sight

I knew she was for me,
She was easy, she had the morals of a man.
I knew she was for me,
She had bleached hair and a miracle bra.
I knew she was for me,
She was interesting, I did all the talking.
I knew she was for me,
She was a nympho, she wanted sex every month.
I knew she was for me,
She said she had a G-spot, I couldn't see it.
I knew she was for me,
She wasn't that fussy about men.
I knew she was for me,
She played hard to get, she ignored me.
I knew she was lesbian,
She was indifferent to me.

I'm Glad I'm A Man
By: A Man

I'm glad I'm a man, you better believe,
I don't live off of yoghurt, diet coke, or cottage cheese.
I don't bitch to my girlfriends about the size of my breasts,
I can get where I want to – north, south, east or west.
I don't get wasted after only two beers
And when I do drink, I don't end up in tears.
I won't spend hours deciding what to wear,
I spend two minutes max fixing my hair.
And I don't go around checking my reflection
In everything shiny from every direction.
I don't whine in public and make us leave early,
And when you ask why, get all bitter and surly.
I'm glad I'm a man, I'm so glad I could sing,
I don't have to sit around waiting for that ring.
I don't gossip about friends or stab them in the back,
I don't carry our differences into the sack.
I'll never go psycho and threaten to kill you,
Or think every guy out there's trying to steal you.
I'm rational, reasonable, and logical too,
I know what the time is and I know what to do.
And I honestly think it's a privilege for me,
To have these two balls and to stand when I pee.
I live to watch sports and play all sorts of ball,
It's more fun than dealing with women after all.
I won't cry if you figure out it's not going to work,
I won't remain bitter and call you a jerk.
Feel free to use me for immediate pleasure,
I won't assume it's permanent by any measure.
Yes, I'm glad I'm a man, a man you see,
I'm glad I'm not capable of child delivery.
I don't get all bitchy every 28 days,
I'm glad that my gender gets me a much bigger raise.
I'm a man by chance and I'm thankful it's true,
I'm so glad I'm a man and not a woman like you!

Things I've Learned In Life

I've learned in life that you cannot make someone love you;
All you can do is stalk them and hope that they give in.
I've learned in life that it takes years to build up trust
Only to have suspicion, not proof, destroy it in a second.
I've learned in life that you can keep puking up
Long after you think you have finished.
I've learned in life that money, not love, gives you hot and steamy passion.
I've learned in life that dysfunctional friends make you feel better
about yourself.
I've learned in life that cocaine is God's way of telling you that you
have too much money.
I've learned in life that a fine is a tax for doing wrong and a tax is a
fine for doing well.
I've learned in life that some people have photographic memories
while other people don't even have the film.
I've learned in life not to eat the yellow snow.
I've learned in life that a day without sunshine is called night.
I've learned in life that change is inevitable, except from a coke machine.
I've learned in life that those who live by the sword get shot.
I've learned in life it is better to be looked over than to be overlooked.
I've learned in life that there are three kinds of people in the world:
those who can count and those who can't.
I've learned in life that you can only be young once but you can be
immature forever.
I've learned in life that the honeymoon is that short period between 'I
do' and 'You better'.
I've learned in life that you cannot be a closet claustrophobic.
I've learned in life that you can't have everything; I mean, where would
you put it?
I've learned not to take life seriously; after all, nobody gets out alive anyway.

Because I'm A Man

Because I'm a man, I must hold the television remote control in my hand while I watch TV. If the thing has been misplaced, I'll miss a whole show looking for it, though one time I was able to survive by holding a calculator in one hand and a mobile phone in the other. In total, I have a remote for the TV, video, DVD, stereo, satellite and one that doesn't actually do anything except give me that placebo feeling.

Because I'm a man, when I lock my keys in the car I will fiddle with a wire clothes hanger and ignore your suggestions that we call a road service until long after hypothermia has set in. Oh, and when the car isn't running very well, I will eventually open the bonnet and stare at the engine as if I know what I'm looking at. If another man shows up, one of us will say to the other, 'I used to be able to fix these things, but now with all these computers and everything, I wouldn't know where to start.' We will then talk stout or beer and discuss football.

Because I'm a man, when I catch a cold I need someone to bring me soup and take care of me while I lie in bed and moan. You never get as sick as I do, so for you this isn't an issue. As a man, I know the meaning of suffering and living with intensive pain and pressure.

Because I'm a man, I can be relied upon to purchase basic groceries at the shops, like milk or bread. I cannot be expected to find exotic items like 'Cumin' or 'Tofu'. For all I know, these are the same thing. And never, under any circumstances, expect me to pick up anything for which 'feminine hygiene product' is an euphemism. I mean, come off it.

Because I'm a man, when one of our electrical appliances stops working I will insist on taking it apart, despite evidence that this will just cost me twice as much once the service man gets here and has to put it back together.

Because I'm a man, I don't think we're all that lost, and no, I don't think we should stop and ask someone. Why would you listen to a complete stranger – how the hell could HE know where we're going? As a descendant of the early Celts, I have the ability to find my way using the stars as a guide, except, that is, if it is cloudy or daytime, then I have to think a lot so I don't need any interruptions or interference.

Because I'm a man, there is no need to ask me what I'm thinking about. The answer is always either sex or football, though I have to make up something else when you ask, so don't. That is why I have to pretend to ignore you sometimes; it's not that I am, it's just that, well, I have to.

Because I'm a man, I do not want to visit your mother, or have your mother come visit us, or talk to her when she calls, or think about her any more than I have to. Whatever you got her for Mothers' Day is OK; I don't need to see it. Did you remember to pick up something for my mother too?

Because I'm a man, I am capable of announcing, 'One more pint and I really have to go,' and mean it every single time I say it, even when it gets to the point that the one bar closes and my mucker and I have to go find another one. I will find it increasingly hilarious to have my pals call you to tell you I'll be home soon, and no, I don't understand why you threw all my clothes into the garden. What's the connection? I mean, what is your problem?

Because I'm a man, you don't have to ask me if I liked the movie. Chances are, if you're crying at the end of it, I didn't. If you're sleeping, then I did.

Because I'm a man, yes, I have to turn up the radio when Bruce Springsteen or The Doors comes on, and then, yes, I have to tell you every single time about how Bruce had his picture on the cover of *Time* and *Newsweek* on the same day, or how Jim Morrison is buried in Paris and everyone visits his grave. Please do not behave as if you do not find this fascinating.

Because I'm a man, I think what you're wearing is fine. I thought what you were wearing five minutes ago was fine, too. Either pair of shoes is fine. With the belt or without it looks fine. Your hair is fine. You look fine. Can we just go now?

Because I'm a man and this is, after all, the twenty-first century, I will share equally in the housework. You do the washing, the cooking, the cleaning, and the dishes. I'll do the rest.

Things I Learn From Baywatch

Some people may be fooled into thinking that Baywatch is uncool,
Lots of beautiful people lazing around a studio pool.
But I watch with interest every plot that unfurls,
Only pervies and sad boys watch it for the girls.

There are some really smart things that appear on the screen,
You soon get to know the contrast between the good and the mean.
You learn a stack from each chartered in-depth plot,
About life and love and all that we're not.

Did you know that Americans spend 15% of their time running slow
motion through the air?
Did you know that you can't trust fat people cause they're unreliable
and have a vacant stare?
Did you know that women with abnormally large breasts are
worshipped as heroes and thinkers?
Did you know that David Hasslehoff once had a car that spoke back
to him but now counsels drinkers?
Did you know that if you live in LA, you will never drown but can be
attacked by jewel thieves and baddies?
Did you know that in LA there's no such thing as grannies?
Did you know that even in intense heat, plastic never melts?
Did you know that in the sun, all you need is your pelt?
Did you know that on the beach, only the crooks are overdressed?
And everybody hugs, desires instant fame or suffers from stress.

Above all these, Baywatch is a metaphor for being,
Life is a beach and not what you're seeing.

I Think I Drowned My Goldfish

Goldie doesn't swim around the bowl anymore.
He just lies at the top of the water on his back,
Looking up at the ceiling in that way.
You know, the same way my Da does when he's drunk,
Or the same way my Ma does when she's not speaking to us,
Or me looking for an elusive answer to my homework.
More so like a dead bird looks at the ground,
Or a petrified tree looks at its roots,
Or a lemming looks standing on the rocks before it jumps.
It is one of those looks that says, 'Please leave me alone;
I'm tired swimming and all I want to do is rest.
Rest forever. Forever in peace. Peace for ever.'
Goldie is digging deeper in our garden now.

All Poets Are Wimps!

They always look at me and say:
'Naw, really. YOU write poetry?'
With a look of sheer disbelief and derision
That's normally tinged with a degree of unnecessary cringing.
You get the feeling that they regret it
The moment the words leave their lips
And that, in response,
They are expecting a crushing blow to the head
Or instant death for daring to challenge my masculinity.
I mean, imagine challenging my masculinity. Me, a real man!
Me, a Creggan man; Me, a real man from Creggan!
A real Creggan man who happens to write.

'Yes, I WRITE POETRY!' I say adamantly.
'Maybe you were expecting a man in tights with long hair
or, perhaps, someone in a smoking jacket with a vacant stare,
maybe a pansy in his button hole?'
'No, no, it's just, well…'
Yeah, I know, I'm not most people's idea
of a 'typical poet' but, then again,
I'm not most people's idea of a typical anything.

I had a hard life, a bad paper round, nits and rickets
And once I had tickets to Seamus Heaney.
But I didn't go; all poets are wimps.

Even the local papers seem to 'mock' me:
'Big Hard Man Turns Poet' the headlines bleat,
Like 'Lorry Driver Does Ballet' or 'Serial Killer Saves Puppy'
Even 'Wrestler Takes Up Knitting'

Why do people associate POETRY, and men who write, with terms like:
Poofs, wimps, loners and weirdos?
What's so 'feminine' about words?

If I utter 'to be, or not to be'
Do I instantly turn homosexual or develop motherly instincts?

If I start wandering, lonely as a cloud,
Does that make me both fluffy and pensive?
Do I lunge to arrange the nearest flowers or talk about stretchmarks?
Sometimes, I wish I could tie my audience up
And, dressed in my best camouflage fatigues and balaclava,
Bellow some of my finest poems at them, Military Drill style.
'Shoulders back, tie that button up,
Now, then, here's rhyming verse you 'orrible little lot.'
Poetry Guerrilla style; Che does rap; Chucky my couplet.
Perhaps then they'll realise that writing poetry
Isn't a weakness; it's a strength, a potent force to be reckoned with.

'YES, I'M A POET' I declare.
'And you'd better like my poems or I might re-arrange your features, boy.
Poetry's for wimps?
Try telling ME that and see what happens!'

If you don't like poetry, YOU'RE the one that's soft.
Fluffy soft.
Fluffy pink bunny soft

You have to be hard to be a poet.
You have to be hard to go deep inside and rummage the emotions.
I might write about that one day.

What you looking at, pussy?
Are you trying to read me?
Me sneer, me leer, me tuff, had enuff, I can be really ruff!

Eddie, 'The Hardman' Poet

What My Ma Taught Me

My Ma taught me the power of anticipation:
    'Just you wait till your Da comes home.'
My Ma taught me about the expectation of receiving:
    'Just you wait until you get home.'
Ma Ma taught me sheer logic:
    'If you fall out of that tree and break your leg, don't come
    running to me.'
My Ma taught me the secrets of medical science:
    'If you don't stop doing that, your eyes will stay like that.'
My Ma taught me about genetics:
    'You're just like your father.'
My Ma taught me about my roots:
    'Do you think we were born in a barn?'
My Ma taught me the power of miracles:
    'Do you think I came up the Foyle in a bubble?'
My Ma taught me how to become an adult:
    'If you don't eat your vegetables, you'll never grow up.'
My Ma taught me wisdom:
    'When you get to my age, you'll understand.'
Above all, my Ma taught me justice:
    'One day you'll have children and I hope they turn out just like
    you. Then you'll see what it's like.'

Ode To Belshaft

You built a big boat, it sunk, get over it.

My Life As It Is

When I was young, I started out with nothing and I still have most of it.
I went to school but I didn't like it, it was full of children acting childish.
I was told the world is my oyster, I mean, have you ever tasted an oyster?
I reckon it was a brave man that ate the first oyster. Come to think of
it, that man was probably a woman who was a man in a previous life.
From an early age I always knew that things come to those that wait
but those things are usually left by the people who got there first and
they are not worth the wait in the first place.
I learned that recent research tells us that three out of four people make
up 75% of the population and that some research causes cancer in rats.
I also learned that 87.5% of statistics are irrelevant.
In my life, I have seen it all, done it all but can't remember most of it.

The Dance Of Eternal Love

You put your right leg in, your left leg out,
Put your dangly bits in and shake them all about.
You do the Karma Sutra and turn me on,
That's what it's all about.
Oh, Karma, Karma Sutra.

*Borrowed from the author of the 'Hokey Cokey' who died quite recently.
They had major difficultly placing him in the coffin – as they put the left
leg in, the left leg came out... etc.*

Sometimes It's Good To Be A Man

I'm glad I'm a man because I get to keep my surname all my life.
I'm glad I'm a man because I'll never have to be a wife.
I'm glad I'm a man because the world is my urinal, I shall not want.
I'm glad I'm a man because every match is a World Cup final.
I'm glad I'm a man because I can arrange my crotch anytime, anywhere, any place.
I'm glad I'm a man because new shoes don't cut, blister or mangle my feet.
I'm glad I'm a man because, to me, chocolate is just another snack food.
I'm glad I'm a man because a well-rendered belch is practically compulsory.
I'm glad I'm a man because I don't care if no one notices my haircut or not.
I'm glad I'm a man because I have one mood all the time.
I'm glad I'm a man because I don't have to wear tights unless absolutely necessary.
I'm glad I'm a man because hot wax never comes near my hairy bits.
I'm glad I'm a man because I'll never experience the pain and joy of childbirth.
I'm glad I'm a man because God made us first, but I suppose practice makes perfect.
And man said to God, 'Why have you made woman so beautiful?' and God says, 'So man would love her.'
And man said to God, 'Why have you made her so stupid?' and God says, 'So she would love you.'
I'm glad I'm a man.
I think, therefore I'm male.

Are You Talking To Me?

'Are you talking to me?' she said alluringly, passing me by.
'Yes, you over there next to the bald-headed guy.'
I said: 'I think you're really hot with that flaming red hair,
It's exceedingly beautiful and really quite rare.

'I love the way it curls around your pretty face,
The way it stumbles almost in a delicate embrace.
The way it darkens the green of your soulful eyes,
The way on your cheek the curls cascade and then lie.'

She took a deep breath as she paused in her stride,
Her lips slowly parted, her eyes open wide.
She smiled as he whipped the wig from his head
'If you like it so much, you can have it instead.'

Ultimate Haiku

The only problem
with Haiku is that
just when you get
started
it's...
Thank you.

Me And Work Have Never Clicked

Me and work have never clicked, never quite got the trick, not that
I'm thick, a bit too quick, on the sick, me.
I never raised a sweat, a bit callous, paintless, workless, shirkless,
penniless, me.

Avoided pain, undue rain, use the brain, rugged terrain, went to Spain, me.
Ignored the hammer, spanner, planner, rather have gigging, not
digging, me.

Once got a job in an orange-juice factory but got canned cause I couldn't
concentrate, not very appealing, same rind every day, gave me the pip.
Once got a job as a lumberjack, but they twigged on, I just couldn't hack
it, got axed, all bark, no oak, no spruce, them tree fellas, or was it four?
After that, got a job as a tailor, it was so-so, but I wasn't suited to it, so
I cuffed it, so button it, mister, says me.
I wanted to be a barber but couldn't cut it, curl up and dye, me.
I could have been a prostitute but had to do a lying week, on my back, me.
Got sacked from the undertaking job for demanding a cost of living rise.
As a doctor, I lost my patients.
In the shoe factory, got the boot, didn't fit in, poor soul, down at heel, me.
As a fisherman, I couldn't live on my net income.
I tried being a witch for a spell but was sacked for cursing, warlocks
to them.
I used to feed giraffes in the zoo but got the sack because I wasn't up to it.
I once got a job in a health club but got the sack because I wasn't fit for
it. I tried swimming pool maintenance but found it was draining, me.
Rosemary the sage told me to work as a herbalist, but I ran out of thyme.
As an electrician the work was shocking, very negative, not positive earth.
As a monk, I was defrocked for having a dirty habit, always led a
cloistered life, me.
I found there was no future in being a historian but that's all in the
past now.
It was a real grind working in a coffee shop with dark, brown roasted
nuts, me.

Life as a lift attendant had its ups and downs, left on Ascension Thursday.
So after all these jobs, I'm no snob, I'll work for my bob, me.
Now I write what I feel, what I see, what I hear, me.
Found my vocation, vacant eyes, pen in hand, dreamy, me.
Now I do what I like, putting people to sleep, creative, me.
Me. I'm happy, 'slap happy', happy, taxidermist, stuff me.

Whatever You Say Is Wrong

'What are you thinking?' she said to him, all suggestively and cuddly.
He was thinking of how warm, caring, wonderful and intelligent she was.
How lucky he was to meet her, light of his life, his reason for life.
'Lies!' said football, 'You're always thinking about football.'
'Do you love me?' she said, testing and provocatively.
Yes is the only answer but he says, 'Who, me? I suppose so.'
'That depends on what you mean, love' or 'Does it matter?' are not good answers.
'Do I look fat in this?' The only answer is 'No.'
You cannot say, 'Compared to what?', 'I've seen fatter' or 'You're not exactly anorexic, are you?'
When asked, 'Is she better looking than me?' you should not say, 'In a different way', 'But you have a nicer personality' or 'Only that she is younger and thinner' as you dice with death.

The Handbag

The woman's handbag is a rare delight, just like Aladdin's cave,
All sorts of things are hidden there, that females like to save,
It's black and big and heavy, with a nice long shoulder strap,
It's weighted down with odds and sods and other stuff like that.
But the lady finds just what she wants deep down amongst her treasure,
Of keys and pins and leg-hair wax and a wooden rule for measure,
The remnants of forgotten ills with aspirins held so dear,
Aromatherapy and rescue remedy with labels quite unclear.
Calorie counters, cotton buds, old lottery tickets too,
Handkerchiefs and white tissues for visiting a foreign loo.
A book of stamps, a tube of glue, letters from I don't know who.
Horoscopes with a personal star, three sets of keys for long-gone car.
Perfume loaded by the box, knitting needles, two pairs of socks,
Bank statements and counterfoils, sachet samples, body oils,
Cassette tapes and eye mascara, postcards from some place in Connemara,
Handbills for keep-fit classes, lipstick and five pairs of glasses,
Emery boards, a pot of Vic, silver tweezers, half a brick,
Screwdriver, spanners, ball of wool, ancient notebook partly full.
A bristle brush for tangled tresses, some photographs and old addresses,
Polo mints and a mobile phone, just in case they stray from home.
Cheque-book stubs, leather gloves, insect spray and assorted rubs,
Driving licence, bingo card, cuttings from the local paper,
Favourite verse, a loaded purse and an broken windscreen wiper,
Credit cards, safety razor, silver buttons off an old blue blazer.
All these things are lugged around and many more as well,
It could be that you need them, you really cannot tell.
But best of all it is a friend, that's with them every day,
Slung upon the shoulder in a very casual way,
And don't forget it is a club – not of the member kind,
But the bag itself when wielded right could change a mugger's mind.

Beaches

There was this man on the beach who calls his dog, dog;
His wife calls him husband and her son calls her mother.
Like the Bisto family, they stroll along in their ignorance that they are
the token ridicule for families less secure in their own gusto.
Middle-income men from middle-class homes with middle-age
paunches inhale and exhale as the bikinis pass by in all directions.
A man fetches a stick that the too-less-than-agile poodle won't;
An overweight woman in too small swimsuit ebbs and flows with the tide
As her much-trodden husband spouse yearns of yachts, thoughts
and wotnots,
He looks for places to hide the body.
Every footprint has a story; even flotsam was wiped clean with moon
moves and jetsam with time;
Wiped like the little boy's drawing of his family on a magic-marker
board, whish, wash, there, all gone, wishful thinking, he thinks.
And the couple who haven't spoken in years use telepathy to glide
across the sand like swallows on the wing – close, but far enough.
Their beautiful toddler of a daughter knows the score and plays the
game; she always wins;
She falls near the spot where her mother buried their first disposable nappy.
Eileen and Tom have lived under the same cloud for years; Tom
doesn't care and Eileen doesn't know.
Here, dog, here. The dog doesn't come.

Lego City

Driving rain in her face, down her back and splashes around
uncovered, unshaven legs,
Balancing precariously on two blocks of cheap leather, knees red with
fake tan running,
Hollywood smile, shiny halter top, doused in perfume, she looks well,
so well, oh so good. Spits out her gum unceremoniously, says it tastes
of Breezer and Regal. Like a prairie dog, her nutritious eyes dart about,
on the juke for her Dream Date.
Dream Date beholds his beauty in the broken pine mirror as his Ma
and Da set upon each other in a living room void of paint and love.
He ignores their taunts as he waxes, lubricates, jells and pouts, beguilingly.
With a wink to the new him, he drops his shoulder, scores a goal and
punches the air just like yesterday, he looks well, so well, oh so good.
She Two wears hooker boots and a top too small for her ego, she is radiant.
She Three isn't feeling well, must have been something she ate, curry
and kulov, a lethal mix, like Red Bull, Schnapps and some German
stuff with gold through it. She loves the way the gold leaf floats
through the liquid like the old Xmas thing with the snow in it, ach,
you know what she means.
Dream Date Two wears torn denims, fake Armani and that oh so too
sweet aftershave.
Dream Date Three is Jack the Lad, is life and soul, a man's man, a
manic knave, next month they'll pull him from a river, still with the
same smirk on his face.
Mother calls him son up, sun down. Porcelain skin translucent and
well defined.
Blue bag city at dead of night, not-so-settled couples like volcanoes,
make their way home. Chips in hand matching the chip on each of
their shoulders. Can't wait to get stuck in. Borstal fodder, line up to
give the dirtiest look, Dirty Harrys every last one. Just like jackals,
scary in a gang, like 'as if you understand'; 'what you looking at, me?';
'let's get one in four, just for the craic.'
The crack of head on pavement or the crack of bone through shirt.
Eerie city at dead of night, urchins shouting, taxis honking, cafés

frying, lonely boy crying, peelers watching as eyes watch peelers, lost man bleeding, couples fighting, dogs barking, mouths abusing, cheeks swelling, promises broken, old man choking. Looking up as the rain falls gently in his face under the street light, seems like anywhere else, it seems like home, long way home, rain cascades from head to toe. CCTV footage makes it look like Chaplin and Buster walk the streets of Lego City.

Ageing Lotharios try to look magnetic under the neon lights, hiding their bald patches, pulling in bellies swollen with beer and watching out for their daughters. Like vultures waiting for the weakest wildebeest to lag behind the pack.

An old man shares a supper with a stray dog. The dog understands his problems but then hunger makes good listeners.

Lego blocks waver from side to side as the twelve-year boy's head grazes the kerb, a crowd gathers as he lies cursing his dead mother's name and his father's shame.

In the laneways, behind shuttered shops selling credit and debt, Dream Date and She wrestle, manipulate, contrive, eat cold pizza and grunt as their parents did before them. They do it well, so well, oh so well. Blue bag city eats its young and renders its kindred obsolete and whiplashed from neglect and arrogance.

She and Dream Date wait for different taxis going back in time, mother and father jive like it's 1975, they won't speak to each other until the crocodile rocks again.

She doesn't feel so good now.

Dream Date kicks a face, he's scored again. He raises his fist in the air as the trolley wheels through A and E gliding past the boy calling for his dead mother and She Three is choking on the tube that saved her life. It was a good night in Lego City, nobody died, so far.

Gone

He is on his chair, waiting to die.
I pass by, he catches my eye.
We wave, he smiles, I confirm.
The world is insignificant, just like him.
No tears will be cried,
No-one shall remember
The lonely old man in the chair
Who sat by that window there
Who passed away last September

Recklessness

Trapped in the dark, you try to find a light
As the darkness closes in and the cold starts to choke you.
You want to give up,
You think to yourself, stop fighting, and give up.
But your heart won't let you
As you struggle and fight on
You finally see the light.

The Theft Of Innocence

How could you know the smell of fear mixed with the taste of beer?

How could you ever know the creak of the stair, the turning of the handle, the sheets gliding over you like a breeze, hands mauling you?

How could you ever know the grinding of hips, biting of lips, the taste of sweat, unwelcome sweat, spilling onto silent tears?

How could you know the sense of shame, to hate your name, the smell of guilt, the fire in vacant eyes, the murmur of climax encased in calloused hand?

How could you know the weight of the baggage I carry, why I cry, drink, freeze when hand touches flesh, when the fine hair on your spine is hurting you?

How would you know the darkness I see when I close my eyes and that blackness is my friend and my enemy?

How would you know? Even if you do care, I was there, where were you?

Fish Down The Barrel

From every angle they aimed at the crowd,
Like shooting fish in a barrel, down the sight
Along the barrel to the foresight, they never had,
Squeeze the adrenalin from the magazine and recoil.
Widowmaker, mother griever, father screamer, sister loss,
Brother silent with plans afoot, baby never knew,
Bodies strewn like leaves from the weeping oak tree.
Rumour said five, reality said fourteen, lies said none,
No damage, no homage, only taigs after all is said and done.
Be prepared, who dare wins, maroon berets coloured like fortified blood.
Havoc reigns, it will take more than thirty years to bury our dead when
the sun shone red the streets ran red, sheets still stain with double sweat
from troubled sleep, reliving death one bright day in winter.

Big Jim

I stared at his face, wrinkled with time and fear,
I thought I saw him smile then shed a single tear.
I knew him all my life, his story, his wife,
I saw a hard, decent worker wade through communal strife.
Thought no wrong of anyone, always lived as the good book says,
He always had a good word on everyone as he bid them time of day.
His words were warnings to keep apart, to keep afar.
Politics kills, he'd often say, learn a trade, forget the war.
Words of wisdom will take you far, sound advice, nurtured from father
to son, generation to generation, keep your head down, well down,
like mine, he said.
Words floated on a breezy wind the day we buried Big Jim.

Sean

Sean found history today.
A crumbled old black and white, frayed at the edges,
One moment frozen in time, a once-in-a-lifetime second.
Twenty-two mud-baked, dirt-caked faces shining,
Forty-three eyes, every dentist's nightmare.
They were ten, maybe nine, all in a line,
World Champions, posing manfully, victorious, precocious boys, all
smiling, loving life.
Boys from hell, fashioned from vitality, assembled for fun,
oblivious to hate,
They laughed at each other and then one to the other
Sean found reality today.
JoJo lost his when only a week older, a drunk man blind
Stevie's castle torched because of what he was.
Five gone with lead ingrained with their names.
Six ceased by their own devices, hooded but resolute,
One didn't even shoot.
Diarmuid melted into a grey mist somewhere, some say LA, some say not.
Michael got bad seed in Holland, ridicule came before death.
Gerard became radical Gearoid, became accountant, became rich,
became Gerard, became indifferent.
Sean became a widow's son, burying his mother and her reminiscences.
Among her precious memories was this snapshot.
Sean found fear today,
Sean found his fears in an old photograph.
Jesus, so did I,
Fourteen down; six to go.

The Ballad Of Terri With An 'I' And Willy With A 'Y'

Through a cloud of steely-blue smoke,
She stood there drinking her vodka and coke.
Surveying the land in search of a bloke,
Finding a mate in Derry was approaching a joke.

Terri looked the part in her six-inch heels,
Exposing her chest as the poker machine deals.
A sip from her glass, 'I'm up for it,' she feels,
Up for a boogie and a few more late-night meals.

Willy stood alone with an Aftershock in hand,
Out for the night and a quick one-night stand.
Supping his pint, he listens to the cover band,
Thinks as he drinks, 'Yes! She'll do me grand.'

The lights were low, the place was a dive,
Most were staring at three couples profound in a jive.
Girls looking for guys who they thought could drive,
While ample bosoms heaved with hormones alive.

Willy swanned through the crowd who gyrated in time,
Nodded to past conquests, they avoiding his shine.
He crossed the dance floor all covered in grime,
Terri stood by the band, she looked so sublime.

It wasn't her fake tan that attracted the man,
It wasn't her fashion, even it appeared somewhat bland.
It wasn't her hair that she moussed with her own hand,
It was the fact that it was his last chance to stand.

'Do you come here often?' he heard himself saying.
She stared at him blankly; a babe for the slaying.
Willy asked, 'What are you thinking; going or staying?'
She giggled, 'A vodka and Red Bull, and I'm really swaying.'

Terri lost her best friend to a brickie from Derry,
Terri lost her virginity on a beach in the Canaries.
Terri lost her front teeth to a bitch up from Kerry,
Terri lost her last lover back to his wife Mary.

Willy lost his dignity against a chip shop wall,
Willy lost his pride just before the fall.
Willy lost his wallet during the last mating call,
Willy lost his respect but was having a ball.

A moment of passion as the two orgasms cry,
He said he'd phone as he zipped up his fly.
She said she'd wait but she knew the lie,
A fling, no ring, no duties, no tie.

They were the perfect couple, that none could despise,
A ready-made family with six wains – no surprise.
A catalogue of debt, two flats and let's surmise
They had each other with tears in their eyes.

The world loves lovers like Terri and Willy,
They all love the one-offs; commitment so silly.
In the back of a Lada or nothing so frilly,
Terri will be out on the prowl in search of her Willy.

'Do you come here often?' says a man called Billy.
'A vodka and Red Bull,' says a blonde girl called Millie.
A thousand couples copulate on sofas and back lanes,
We'll be back next Friday for more of the same.

There ain't no ugly people after 2.00am, or so the song says.
There ain't no dignity after 2.00am, or so my mother says.
There ain't no viginity after 2.00am, or so my brother says.
A pizza, a vodka and Viagra, who cares if they stay.

Glenbrook

'I'm up to here wae yer squealing and bitching,
Give my head peace,' she roared from the kitchen.
'Me Ma was right, you couldn't be civil,
Sitting there wae the face of a devil.'

'Go boil yur head, yer polluting the air.'
'Come out and say that and that's a dare.
You've not got the balls, yer feared of a fight.
Just sit there, ya blaggard, yer talking auld shite.'

Sundays in me granny's was where I was raised,
Warm exchanges of words by a fire that blazed.
They lived together for sixty-odd years,
Through all the laughter, the debt and the tears.

Words that strangled, bruised and cut,
Doors that banged loudly, open and shut.
Two razor-sharp tongues that lashed and bashed,
Two egos in turmoil lay battered and bruised.

Like a verbal ping pong game where a point is a name,
They roared like good-oh the aim is to shame.
Never mind the neighbours, the dog or the wains,
Every Sunday was always the piggin' same.

After six hours of roaring and shouting,
Folded arms and lips apouting.
Wagging fingers and dirty looks that linger,
They go to the pub where my granny's a singer.

They laugh and they joke over brandy and coke,
They sit at the bar where they'd point and they'd poke.
They walk home arm in arm, causing no harm,
By breakfast time they raised the alarm.

As they got older, they got no wiser,
She took to bed and he couldn't rise her.
They roared up the stairs to wake one another,
Till their deathbed, they were always in bother.

I remember the day that he passed away,
I fought back the tears, didn't know what to say.
She looked at the man who thought was her master,
Smiling, she said: 'Look at ye now, y'auld bastard.'

She cried the day he was put in the ground,
What'll she do, now that he's not around?
She followed him soon to a place far away,
I can hear them now as each has their say.

Texas Man

I met a man at a bar, who told me wasn't the war in Ireland sad.
In his slow Texan drawl he said it was a throwback to the bad old days
when blaggards, scoundrels and evil ruled his native land, although he
hadn't been there, he saw the Quiet Man twice, not so nice.

I thought for a while and was about to tell him about Cromwell, how
famine decimated half our people, about Bobby Sands, Bloody
Sunday, about the coffin ships, internment, ritualised hatred,
intimidation, sectarianism, gerrymandering, 4-inch plastic bullets.

I was about to tell him about how friends had floated in their own
blood, children standing incomprehensively at the scene of their
daddy's murder, the fears of being a parent, mass saturation, terror,
the smell of death, smoke, cortex, Semtex, burning flesh, palpable
taste of fear.

I was about to tell him about being second class, unequal, no
confidence, anger, resentment and rejection.

I was about to tell him, but all I said was, 'Yes, it is.'

Brooke Park

Victorian laid pathways crisscross the blueprint for opulence
Where urchins sought shelter, food and solutions,
Where dogs now defecate, growl and couple while owners sit in Astras
reading in-depth articles on pollution.
On bleak winter days, fresh spring pampas, late summer evenings,
amid autumnal colours and discarded spliffs and fags.
Flowerbed trampled by budding Beckham bends
As ageing Lotharios sprawl amongst a sea of blue bags.
Sure-foot toddlers spin round and round, a dizzy send-off
By the brushes there he made his first pass
Amongst the maple trees and the broken glass
Where the Black Man statue stands and repels
And the weeping willow remembers better spells.
Broken swings, cast away things, lone voice sings,
A pensioner scurries through the park to lock her door.
Stay in the dark as stray dogs bark and Victorian souls wonder what
went wrong with this wonderful park.

Johnny The German

Johnny the German lives on our street.
He stands at his window every night
Looking at the moon wondering
If he will ever see another winter
Or if he'll open the door to his son
Or if he falls down will someone hear him cry out
Or will he sleep, never to waken to the dawn chorus
Or will he be able shout at the TV during the football
Or if he'll ever see the day through without his pills.
Johnny the German stands at his window wondering
If the people he waves to will ever wave back.
Nobody waved the day Johnny stopped looking at the moon.

Monologues
And Musings

A Rant On The Mobile Phone

Don't you just hate the mobile phone and what it has done to human evolution?

Never underestimate the power of stupid people, especially in large groups. Walk down any street in any city, in any village in any town and you'll see them. Thousands of them. Lips aquiver, roaring into their wrists.

There should be a specific place where people should only be allowed to answer these evil seeds of the devil. People on mobile phones in public places irritate me. They are the same people who point to their wrist when they ask you the time. The same people if they lose the remote control will stare blankly at the mundane on television rather than change the channel manually. But I have never trusted telephones anyway. In the elaborate wardrobe of human emotions, mobile phones are the ugly tank top.

I've always known that there are stupid people in our society. Even when I was a teenager, I knew that most adults were dumb. Once when I was a teenager, a wet, hungry, cold and alone teenager in Dublin, I was trying to get through to Derry with a 'Mammy help me' call. Standing in a dodgy-looking backstreet phone box, I had to endure a lesson in political correctness when the telephone operators in the North and the South argued whether the phone call was to Londonderry or Derry. At that stage it could have been in Outer Mongolia as far as I cared. I was left hanging on the telephone. I was having enough problems not knowing how to wind up the phone or press button A or B. A salutary lesson was learned. Never trust the tank tops. But then the world is rife with tank tops. I was at the opening of a play recently, and, almost in unison, the Hallo Henrys decided to pollute the auditorium with intermittent renditions of the *Bumblebee, Mexican Hat Dance* and *Crocodile Rock.* Some people have no consideration. Not only do they interrupt a great performance but also they pollute the air with trash music.

Mobile phones are dangerous. Mobile phones are dangerous in the hands of stupid people. But most of all mobile phones are dangerous to stupid people. I remember sitting outside a café in New York and counting eleven people in forty minutes who were so engrossed on the phone that walked straight into a tree (*Homer says Doah!)*

'But what would I do without it?' you ask. I'll tell you what you did before mobiles, faxes, email, text messages, pagers, voice mail and the phone that looks like a hamburger. My forefathers (not that I had four fathers, if you know what I mean), my ancestors, used to wave at each other. They would send smoke signals, use sign language, write to each other, draw on cave walls and even talked face-to-face. Imagine that, people actually sat face down and talked, exchanged words, faced each other and communicated one-on-one. Sounds so old fashioned now, doesn't it? The next time you are out for a drink, a meal, a walk along the riverside, take a look around you. Feeding frenzies on the phone. Couples staring blindly into space as they communicate to invisible friends. Not talking to each other but to other people elsewhere.

How would *Sylvia's Mother* be famous if mobile phones were about then? Whoever said that talk was cheap? I've always believed that a phone bill is a tax on talking. But then I agree with bigger phone bills. Bigger phone bills should cut down the length of time talking on the phone and encourage more face-to-face communications. When it was just one phone company, it was simple: we just moaned about that one company. But since deregulation, we have too many to moan about. Ordinary phone bills are bad enough but mobile phone bills are the goose bumps of scary things. It wouldn't be too bad but in some places along the border you can walk from your kitchen to the living room and have to pay international rates.

Using the phone is a gender thing anyway. Men use the telephone as a communication tool to send short messages to each other. The conversation tends to consist of sharp grunts and noises mixed with a number of 'Aye, right', 'Wise up', 'Your sister...' and 'Three-nil' utterances. However, a woman can talk to her friend for three hours with neither of them taking a breath or even listening to what the other says. And when you inquire what the contents of the conversation were about you'll be told, 'Ach, nothing much.' Then the phone rings again and the whole ritual goes into round two.

But I suppose if you want the latest in modern technology you have to pay for it. I mean, if you really want a videophone on your wrist with WAP facilities and have the money to pay and maintain it, go for it, sad boy. But don't come crying to me when you've walked into a tree, offended everyone in the theatre, fallen out of love with your partner, been abandoned in Dublin when your battery is flat and everyone calls you a tank top. Don't you just love a moan about the phone!

However, I am man enough to acknowledge that the world has also benefited from the invention of the telephone. If it weren't for the phone, we would never have found out how crooked Richard Nixon was. We would never know what it is like to receive a call from a double-glazing salesman just as the match goes to sudden death. And what would lonely wee men do without Premium phone lines? David Dunseith would just be another shock jock. What would we leave on the counter of the pub instead of the obligatory mobile phone? Ironically, I even heard of a telephone hotline that exists for people who have a fear of using the telephone. Work that one out.

If you need to talk to someone about any of the issues raised in this rant, please phone Someone Who Really Cares. I have a new hotline number: 0800 See If I Care.

I Want To Be Six

To Whom It May Concern:

I am hereby officially tendering my resignation as an adult in order to accept the responsibilities of a six-year-old. I want to be six again.

I want to go to McDonald's and think it's the best place in the world to eat. I want to sail sticks across a fresh mucky puddle and make waves with rocks. I want to think M&Ms are better than money because you can eat them. I want to play football during break time and stay up late on Christmas Eve waiting to hear Santa and Rudolph on the roof. I want to play alla balla, who's got the ball?; red light, green light; cheevies; 20-a-side football with 36 goals each half and the next goal the winner. I want to eat Black Jacks and make my teeth and tongue go black. I want to read about heroes and villains under the sheets with a torch. I want to write a letter to Roy of the Rovers and join the Melchester United fan club. I want to lie back on the wet grass and look up at the funny faces in the clouds.

I want the right to stamp my feet and cry if I don't get my way and shut up when I get a clip from an adult hand. I want to smell the distinct aroma of newly baked apple cakes, run my finger around the bowl and steal the inside of the pie. I want to hunt the present in the house. I want to sleep in whatever way I want. I want to laugh out loud at the antics of the Bash Street Kids, Dennis the Menace, and Korky and be enthralled with the deeds of Dan Dare, Spiderman and Superman.

I long for the days when life was simple. When all you knew were colours, the addition tables and simple nursery rhymes. It didn't bother you because you didn't know what you didn't know, and you didn't care.

I want to go to school and have snack time, breaks, playtime, and field trips. I want to be happy because I don't know what should make me upset. I want to think the world is fair, and everyone in it is honest and good. I want to believe that anything is possible. In this world, everything is good.

Somewhere over time, I learned too much. I learned of war, prejudice, rape, starving and abused wains, sectarianism, lies, unhappy marriages, debt, illness, pain and mortality. I want to be six again. I want to think that everyone, including myself, will live forever because I don't know what death is.

I want to be oblivious to the complexity of life, and be overly excited by the little things again. I want television to be something I watch for fun, not something I use for escape from the things I should be doing. I want to live knowing the little things I find exciting will always make me as happy as when I first learned them...I want to be six again.

In those formative years, an application was applying for employment, a programme was a TV show, a cursor swore, a keyboard was a piano! Memory was something that you lost with age. A logon was adding wood to a fire. A hard drive was a long trip on the road. A mouse pad was where a mouse lived. A web was a spider's home. And a virus was the flu!

I remember not seeing the world as a whole, but rather being aware of only the things that directly concerned me. In my world, my Da was the hero, my mother the nurse, cook, social worker and lawyer. I want to be naive enough to think that if I'm happy, so is everyone else. I want to walk down the beach and think only of the sand beneath my feet, and the possibility of finding that blue piece of sea glass I'm looking for. Maybe finding a straw for that frog, putting bees in a bottle, clasping butterflies between chocolate covered fingers, pulling the one leg of a Daddy Long Legs. Life would become so much of an anticlimax once you find out that you weren't swapped at birth in the hospital or found under a gooseberry bush and definitely not brought by the stork.

I want to spend my afternoons climbing trees and riding my bike, letting the grown-ups worry about time, where the food comes from, the appointment at the dentist, and how to find the money to fix the old car. I want to wonder what I'll do when I grow up, and what I'll be, whom I'll be, and not worry about what I'll do if this doesn't work out. I want that time back. I could be whatever I wanted to be. I could fly in space, climb the highest mountains, dive in the deepest seas, save the last tiger in the world and keep it as my pet. I could be shot, count to ten, and get up again.

I want to see how many chips I can get into my mouth at the one time, see how long I can hold my breath for, scratch until I go really red, play Kerby until the sun sets, eat sweets until I want to be sick, shout at the picture screen, sit by the window, hide the Brussels sprouts under the table, pick scabs, tempt the neighbour's dog, put the cat in the bin, climb the drainpipe, pretend my Ma was alien and then plan the invasion of her alien planet. I would be proficient in her alien language and I would trick them into a big deep pit where a special secret thing would do something I didn't understand and kill all the alien people with five eyes, three arms and a big green trunk. That would be so cool and dead easy for a space traveller like me.

Life should be an escape, so that when my computer crashes, or I have a mountain of paperwork, or depressed friends, or a fight with someone special, or my father's death, or bittersweet memories of times gone by, or second thoughts about so many things, I can travel back and build a snowman without thinking about anything except whether the snow sticks together, and what I can possibly use for the snowman's mouth. And how your friends are your muckers and your muckers would help you kill that big thing with the long green trunk that lives under your bed.

I want to be six again. Do you?

Yours faithfully
Eddie Kerr
Aged 42 and a half.

No Mo' Gallagher's Blues

I was reared (some would say half-reared) in Melmore Gardens in the lower half of the Creggan Estate. Well, to be more precise, the Broadway end of the street. I often tell people in the theatre world that I was in Broadway long before I started writing plays.

From the moment I was born, I knew that we knew we were different. Not in terms of wealth, power or status but importantly, we, the people of the Broadway end of Melmore, had pebble dash houses. This gave us a smack of influence and a sense of pride within the estate. Leenan Gardens to Beechwood had red brick, Bligh's Gardens had flats, the mad mile had cement-fronted houses, High Park didn't want to belong to the estate so, therefore, we knew we were different. In other cities in more affluent countries, this would be a sign of rich suburbia but not with us. We knew we weren't better, just different. We were different because we were self-sufficient. We were a kingdom, our own little world, outside the Pale, outside the norm and beyond the realms of exterior influences.

We had a breadman who would sell us a rake of buns for a tanner, even if most of them were stale. I can still taste the mouldy Nikki cakes and Chester bread. They say that single parents are a recent phenomenon but back then, any man who had the semblance of a trade worked away in England and a perpetually pregnant women reared the wains. Obviously the letters they wrote in those days were much more romantic than the emails and text messages of today. You could say that it was pregnancy by extrasensory perception.

We had a man who would drown a litter of pups or kittens in a bucket for the price of five Woodbine. We had four dockers who seldom appeared to work except on a Friday, late into the early hours of the morning. We had a man who never said anything during all the time I lived there. He nodded but never spoke, not even to his wains. He would walk down the street, smiling and nodding at everyone but never uttered a word or a syllable. I thought he was dumb or suffered from some mysterious illness that only Lourdes could cure. But he mesmerized us wains. We would sneak up behind him, bump into him, shout vile obscenities at him. We would do anything just to get a verbal reaction. All he ever did was smile and nod. Once, in a final act of desperation I asked his son why his Da never spoke and he just smiled, nodded in my direction and walked away. I never knew why and still don't know now, even to this day.

I even asked my Da the reason for this affliction but he just smiled, nodded and walked away as well. Watching him walk away, my Ma said maybe he was like every other Derry man, he was waiting for something intelligent to say.

We had a midwife-cum-undertaker-cum-witchdoctor. She was the first unofficial home-help service I ever met in my life. She often said it didn't matter to her if they were coming or going or couldn't come or go, she would soon sort them out with a bucket of warm water and a flannel made from a Tillie's sheet. She could deliver a wain, lay out a corpse or cure the flu, all with the full-length ash of a well-sucked Park Drive balanced delicately at the corner of her mouth. It wasn't her obviously well-honed skills that drew gasps of amazement from us wains; it was her ability to do her work, conduct an incessant and never-ending conversation, and not breathe that dazzled us. Whether it was an umbilical cord, death shroud or whooping cough, she could go through the motions without dropping even a flicker of ash. In all my time watching her, I never even saw her light a new fag but merely maintain the extended ash of the everlasting one. You can be sure anyone who could master this obvious skill was worth admiring. I've seen impostors since but they could not hold a candle (or an ash) to her. (As an aside, I once saw my own granny drop the entire contents of her sucked-out Parkie into the Sunday soup, smile at me, stir it vigorously and no-one was the wiser.)

If that woman were alive now she would probably have her own private practice sorting out the real and imagined ailments from a myriad band of malingerers. She was one of three old women who wore long black dresses, regardless of the weather, and never appeared to sleep. No matter the season of the year or the time of day, the three would be sitting up all hours talking, smoking, rumouring and castigating their menfolk. They were also renowned for their ability to down more stout in one night than all of Garvan's pubs put together.

We also had a man who would – and did on many occasions – fight at the drop of a hat. This was usually his own as he tripped on the footpath on his way home from a night on the barstool.

But above all, we had Bert. Bert was older than we were. He was braver than we were. He could let three ferrets run up and down the legs of his best Burton's suit on a Sunday – while he was still in it! Bert was hairier than we were. He had sideburns before they became fashionable with the Kinks and Beatles. Bert had a tattoo. As with all tattoos, there was a history to it.

A dark story from a shady past. It was embellished during an overnight stay in Bundoran; the tattoo was etched with Indian ink and carved into his right arm just below the elbow. It said Fillymena (spell it out). The story goes that he was drunk, met a girl called – yes, you've got it – Philomena, fell in love, got the tattoo and split up before the ink was dry and he realised her name was spelt wrongly. There was something special, mysterious even, about a girl who could do that to the likes of Bert.

But Bert was something else. He was the man amongst boys. Three times as old, three times our size and a third less our IQ, Bert was not the sharpest knife in the drawer. But when other gangs from Leenan, Malin, Dunmore, Dunree or Central would try to mess us about, we could always call on the services of Big Bert. Without pomp and ceremony, Bert would appear from the mist of the smoky chimneys like a true Celtic warrior, descend on the marauding foes and banish them unceremoniously from our turf. This was the story time after time, invasion after invasion. We would do the running, Bert would do the standing.

That was grand until he met his match with Bobby B, who, with just several moves of his eyes, reduced Bert to a crying and sniveling heap. Even though Bobby B was half Bert's age, he was our hero now. No-one told Bert that Bobby was big into judo three times a week at a club behind Maddens in Queen Street. He went to every class for the last six weeks so he was bound to be a black belter by then. Defeated and vanquished, Bert became the butt of that cruel humour that shreds your confidence and reduces you to a communal laughing stock. It always amazes me how fickle Derry wans can be. One slight whisper can be the difference between being a hero or a villain. Almost overnight, Bert the erstwhile majestic Celtic warrior, soon became Bert, the simple village idiot. Simple Bert moved away a week later. He went to his aunt in England. Rumour has it he joined the Metropolitan Police. Yes, we are ashamed to say it but there may be a Melmore man working to keep law and order on the streets of Islington or Putney.

It was your average Melmore, Creggan, Derry family setup although a bit on the small side. There were six of us in a two-bedroom house. My Ma claims that she moved into the house when there weren't even stairs in it. For years she thought we lived in a bungalow. It was your average family menu: stews on Mondays, Wednesdays and Saturdays; skirts (pork) on Tuesdays, fish on Fridays and meat and two veg on Sundays. It was your average Melmore childhood: 33-a-side football. We used to insert straws into frogs we found out in the quarry and blew them up with a glee of delight. We walked out to the Black Hut at the back of Creggan to buy Danny Boy caramels and played cheevies through the jungle of hedges and gardens. We held major spitting and pissing competitions between us all, stole rhubarb from auld Maggie's backyard, and played knick-knock at dusk. Kerby in the rain, short trousers and sloppy joes, muggy summer nights collecting half a rainforest for the bonfire on the 15th night, slagging, crying, fighting, laughing, dreaming, scheming, believing and stealing kisses, apples and the limelight. Innocence rules the streets.

Then 1968 came and went. Rumours abounded that something wasn't right. We shall overcome. Angry heads vying for an audience, negotiating a defence, students in some other far-off place, black people in other countries, one man one vote, houses and jobs. 'One man getting the vote, what about the rest of us?' shouted big Willie at the black-and-white television parked precariously on a rickety table. We had a house. Sure everybody in our street had a house, otherwise they couldn't live there. A job; sure half the men in our street had jobs across in Burnley or Bradford or Birmingham. Sure didn't they come home every June and Christmas to prove it? Right enough, a lot of men didn't work, couldn't find work, and when they did work, the factories closed before they could make a rise. Sure most mothers worked in the house, all hours of the night, doing collars and buttonholes for the factory agents.

We'll walk hand in hand. What is all the fuss about? My Ma always shouted: 'Here we go again.' Go where again? I didn't know, nobody told me for years where we were going until I worked it out for myself, and I'm still not sure. It wasn't until years later I was told that when I was a mere bump in the womb I became a pre-natal victim of the 'here we go again' syndrome. During the 1950s campaign, at seven months pregnant, my Ma was caught up in a baton charge and ended up lying in a heap in the doorway of Gallagher's Family Butchers, Purveyors of Quality Meats and Poultry, in Sackville Street. And it was only when I got into a fracas with a member of the Anglian regiment that I learned my Uncle Tony had been involved in a similar row with a B-man two decades before for shouting 'Up the Rebels'. I'm still not sure where we are going but my wains shout 'Up the Ra'.

I was a ball boy in the Brandywell the day my Da and brother were beat down Duke Street and over the bridge. It was only when I got home to an empty house, and just after Kenneth Wolstenholme told me how Celtic had done, that the house became abuzz with excitement. Black eyes shining in the twilight, wounded pride and arrogant threats about revenge and the 'here we go again' scenarios lambasting our living room. My brother had a trophy, a well-battered and bruised shield liberated from a fallen peeler. The same type of shield I had seen in McKane's attic one night we were playing hide and seek. It matched the uniform their Da wore as he left the house every Tuesday and Thursday night when a black Morris Minor beach wagon picked him up and took him out past Brae Head.

By 1970 the street had started to change. It was a dividing line. Many of our neighbours came and went. David and Norman left to a flood of tears and promises. What was going to happen now? How would things ever be the same again? This was more than just an average childhood friendship. These were friends that you would die for, kill for and stand up for. They didn't know they were leaving until the last moment. But we knew they were going. Their Ma told my Ma who told Gerry's Ma who told us. We didn't tell them. It wasn't our place to tell them. Anyway, I always knew they were different: they liked the Beatles and I liked the Stones. They marched on the 12th and I didn't. They went to Sunday school and I didn't. Their family wanted to leave, ours didn't. They felt scared, we didn't. They felt safer across the bridge, we didn't. Isn't it funny how things seldom change? Throughout my life, I have always felt 'here we go again'. I hope my children never have to say that.

I'm Tired Of...

Somebody said to me once that when one door closes another just slams in your face. That's the way my life has always been. Sometimes I get really tired hearing how terrible I am, how difficult life is and how lucky I am to have all these people to care about me. I guess I don't know how lucky I am. That's my problem; I have been dogged by luck all my life.

I'm really tired of being told that I don't measure up to unrealistic expectations. Whose expectations? Certainly not mine. I am told to act my age and then sent to my room for asking questions.

I am tired of people assuming the outcomes of my life before I have had a chance of living it. I am tired of all the lectures and the patronising smiles. I am bored with the whisperings and the outright condescending remarks. I am tired of being told that I exaggerate the truth and over-dramatise things that are really important to me.

I am tired of having my conversations taped, written down, videoed, recorded, edited, duplicated, reported, circulated, assessed, evaluated and monitored, and still no-one listens to what I am actually saying.

I need to be heard. I have a voice. I have words to say. I have feelings to share. So many people telling me what to do and no-one listens to a word I say. So many people telling me where to go, where not to go, how to do it, how not to do it, who I can talk to, who I can't talk to. When I question, I am a troublemaker. When I am troubled, I am ignored. When I want, I am greedy. When I don't want, I am given. When I am surrounded, I am isolated. When I am alone, I am remote. When I want my space, I am a misfit. When I need help, I am abandoned. When I need to be secure, I am violated. When I want to be me, I am told to change and adapt.

At some point in our lives we can see the real difference between theory and practice. We know when the system has failed us and we have supposedly failed the system. We know when things work and don't work. It's really hard when your identity becomes a caseload and the load becomes too heavy, especially for the only care worker that tries to help me or the one who really cares. Sometimes one person can make a difference but you quickly come to the conclusion that person is usually me.

When my life and my individuality become a number on a file, I feel it. It's like sitting on a roundabout watching new faces come and go and offer no solution to help or resolve my problems. Does a job description include a moral obligation to me, the person? Does their training include actually hearing what I say?

When they come across me for the first time, that look, as they read the file. You know that look. Notes on a page telling tales of misunderstandings, bouts of immaturity, lessons learned. Stories of things gone by, of lives past and long dusted. Words like rejection, difficult, selfish, argumentative, arrogant, spring to their mind. Please listen to what I am saying, spring to *my* mind. If there are two sides to every story, I have a say! Not every word in a file is right, nor are the people who write in them always right. Teachers, Counsellors, Educational Welfare Officers, Social Workers, Doctors, Behavioral Psychologists, Therapists, Psychiatrists, Advisors, Assessors. Too many people, not enough care. Bombarded with concepts, clichés reprimands and faces.

I am as angry as the day I came into care but my anger is more restrained, directed, controlled. You would think by now life would have sucked my confidence away but I feel strong. I know I am a stronger person, even though I feel powerless to make decisions about my life.

Do as I say, not as I do. Do as we say, not as we do. Don't do anything. Let us decide what has to be done. Let us decide. I won't be here next week; a student will be here in my place. It was really interesting working with you. I am being transferred. I was ill. Trust me, it's for the best. You have to try better. She left last week. I'll phone you next week with the answer. Even a care worker can be ill. What's your problem? Well, I'm telling you I have to. Of course I have holidays. What's your goal in life? Phone me tomorrow. I hear what you're saying. Of course I care. Do you not realise it's Friday afternoon? I would if I could but I can't. Budget. You will have to sort yourself out. Where were you? I can section you. Grounded. Until you prove otherwise, that's the way it will be.

I am tired of excuses, queues and new faces. I am just tired, so very tired. But then again, so are you.

Eulogy To Oscar Lewis

I have long admired the work of American photojournalist G Tod Slone, who has worked extensively in Third World countries as well as in the underbelly of Americana. Last year, he published a number of storybook essays about his trips through Central and Latin America. I have never been to these places but have always had empathy for the poor and downtrodden in all continents, including here on our own island. I penned the following as a result of looking beyond the lens into the eyes of those pictured in the photographs. The following comes from my interpretation of what I perceive and feel about what I see in Slone's photographs. As a student of anthropology (honestly), I have always been inspired by the work of Oscar Lewis, who developed the theory of the 'Culture of Deprivation'.

In our society, children are corralled behind steel-linked fences with peering eyes so careful of intruders, suspicious of intentions and watchful of strangers. We have developed secure doors, vetting systems and watchful eyes to protect our future inheritors.

On the streets of Slone's Mexico, the street urchins of the *zocalo*, the *golfillos*, are the serfs of the streets who pay homage to the American dollar. Out of the effects of poverty, necessity will clean your shoes, carry your bag, give you directions, sell you dancing dolls, smile for the camera and give a head to pat. A *peso* goes a long way when you are hungry and your baby brothers are even hungrier and your mother needs medicine and a drunkard of a father needs more. Amid tourist havens, gazebos look wonderful in the camera's eye, like placebos to conscience; they are replete with flowers and scent. Shoe shiners polish their faces in dusted leather. The aroma of almond, brazil and sunflower wafts through the air in a pungent stream to be inhaled and savoured. The *artesonias* sell their wares amid gossip, slander and swearing. On sale are obtuse wooden animals carved from a copal tree. Raised on a diet of *chapulines* (fried grasshopper), the vendors smile easy. Who said that money and happiness go together?

Some babies drink from puddles, much to the horror of Marge and Herb from Wisconsin. They look like they have a constant bad smell in their nostrils. But regardless, they haggle with the child's mother for another peso less below price. The constant crying of the children settles the price and the cost of poverty means 'sell', even though it is at a loss. Marge and Herb smile as they claim another bargain to cram into an already stuffed suitcase. The children live on the streets, pee openly where they stand, eat alfresco and sleep contently in the shadow created by the nut vendor's stall. Maybe before they sleep they will receive manna from above as the nuts fall in their direction. When they aren't hustling, sleeping, eating, crying, fighting, swearing or selling, they play.

All except the boy with the limp; his mother ties a rope around his good leg but he seldom makes the rope tight. He looks at the children playing. He watches them as they devise a new game with a half a football as the treasure. He is beyond being jealous and laughs with them as they make the rules up as they go along. Even though the children tease him, he knows they are only teasing for fun. He spends so much time laughing that some older people have questioned his sanity. But most of the time his laughter is ubiquitous. He also laughed loudly the day a *gringo* ruffled his hair and called him amigo; as if he would be... so ridiculous. So ridiculous that just the thought of it would make him smile.

The rest of the children play as children should play. They play by expressing their imagination, playing together. No need for designer toys, square cubed electronic whizzers, without expensive broken unbreakables. There is no need for satellite television in every room of the place you call home. You can't run to the fridge just because you are thirsty or hungry or need a blast from the sugar in junk food. Roles are very precise. The rules are simple. When you are poor, you know your place. You know what you have to do to survive. You will do what you have to do to make your family survive another day in abject and relative deprivation. You sew the footballs that millionaire footballers kick, you cut the cloth that makes the designer top you see in the magazines, you file the rhinestones that make the shirt that the singer wears on television when he sings the songs of broken hearts and lonely homes.

A movie star once stopped at the square as he made his way to the movie set where he was to play a leader of the revolution that brought freedom to the village. His nose was still white from the gringo snuff he snorted. He wanted to take the sister of José the barber away in his long black limousine. She was twelve. Her mother said no, her father said maybe. Maria said nothing, as she was not asked. The movie star drove away without her, leaving the sound of her crying as her father beat her again. The movie star died alone in a motel. They found him with a spike coming out of his arm and immersed in his own urine. He was dead for over three weeks and no-one noticed. His funeral made the teatime news in 230 countries. His latest movie is a hit. Maria lost an eye when her father beat her the night before her namesake's feast day.

The little girl approached the bloated stockbroker from the mid-town penthouse who earns more per day than the entire village earns in a year. She showed him a tray of *chicles*. *'Fifty centavos cada uno,'* (a dime for each one) she said. He looked at the sadness in her face and the hope etched in her olive eyes. He took four boxes from the tray and gave her two pesos. *'No,'* she protested, *'fifty centavos cada uno.'* The stockbroker put the boxes back and gave her the two pesos but still she protested vehemently: *'No, senor, fifty centavos cada uno.'* He gave her one peso and took two boxes; she smiled triumphantly and moved on to the next customer. The stockbroker stood bewildered, unsure of what this salutary lesson was. He spends his life wallowing in greed and corruption and feels humbled by the little girl selling chicles.

A new bus arrived in the square, the mariachi band raises the tempo and more burning tourists arrive to be harried by the golfillios and vendors. Like piranhas, the urchins surround their prey before selecting the prime suspects. The children were already experts in their trade by the age of seven. They could read the tourist face as if it were a road map to survival. By six, they were well schooled in the art of parting a tourist from their easily acquired wealth. An overweight female wrestler from Athens, Georgia, became the focal point for the older children as the younger ones used her bulk as a Hula Hoop. She spun around and around until she became quite nauseous and the joke was no longer funny. The older boy called, *'Nada mas!'* and there was nada mas. Relieved, the wrestler sat on the wall that surrounds the square and wiped her forehead. Flustered, she checked her handbag for her purse and cards; all was well. She breathed a sigh of relief and waddled over to join the rest of her tour group.

The summer months were bizarre. Hundreds of tourists would disembark from the air-conditioned buses, many oblivious to the plight of the golfillas. What they could see, they couldn't feel. What they couldn't feel wouldn't cost them anything. Conscience and morality are cheap; a mere few pesos can solve both. The children were branded with the scar of odium. The tourist was branded with the scar of wealth and relative choice. Poverty does not offer choices. Poverty does not offer hope. As the air-conditioned coach pulled away from the square, the boy with the limp never looked up as he watched the ants work effortlessly in the noonday sun; everyone works hard to etch a living in the square. Everyday is a work day, no holidays for the poor. Another bus arrives and a new chapter commences again.

It's A Funny Old World

Things That Make Me Go Hmmmmmm

I've often sat and wondered
About those things that make me ponder
About the world we live in.
How these things we call words can make us smile, angry, hurt, cry
And sometimes lead to sin.
But the world in all its glory
Helps me tell the story
And allows me to look in quiet quandary
At the things that we say...

If you live in Australia, do you call the rest of the world the 'up over'?
Why is it that day breaks and night falls?
Can you buy an entire chess set in a pawnshop?
If blind people wear dark glasses, why can't deaf people wear earmuffs?
If cats and dogs had no fur, would you still pet them?
If space is a vacuum, who empties the bag?
If you spin a Chinese man round ten times, would he become disorientated?
The main reason why Santa is happy is because he knows where all the bad girls live.
I believe that five out of four people have problems with fractions.
If man evolved from apes, why do we still have apes?
Do infants enjoy infancy as much as adults enjoy adultery?
Why isn't eleven pronounced onety-one?
If 'I am' is the shortest sentence in the English language, is 'I do' the longest sentence?
If lawyers are disbarred and clerics defrocked, are cowboys deranged, electricians delighted, musicians denoted and tree surgeons debarked?
If a pig loses its voice, does it become disgruntled?
Are part-time bandleaders called semiconductors?
If a jogger could run at the speed of sound, would he still hear his Walkman?
Why is it called lipstick when the lips can still move?
How can there be 'self-help' groups?
How many screwdrivers does that boy Phillip own?
If marriage were outlawed, only outlaws would have in-laws.

If they throw rice at weddings in America, do they throw hamburgers in China?

Is boneless chicken an invertebrate?

Will all those who believe in psychokinesis raise my hand?

The early bird might get the worm but the second mouse always gets the cheese.

Does the little mermaid have to wear an algae-bra?

Before they invented drawing boards, what did they go back to?

A clear conscience is usually a sign of a bad memory.

Talk is cheap, that's why supply exceeds demand.

When you swim in a lake and an eel bites your bake, that's a moray.

If you lined up all the cars in the world end to end, there'd still be some eejit with Donegal plates who'd try and pass them all.

If light travels faster than sound, is that why some people look brighter than they sound?

Stressed spelt backwards is desserts.

I believe that politicians and nappies should be changed regularly for the same reasons.

The word politics comes from the Greek word 'poly', meaning many, and 'ticks', irritating little insects that annoy people.

Everyone should practise safe eating, always use the right condiments.

Brain cells come and brain cells die but fat cells live for ever.

You don't stop laughing because you grow old but you can grow old because you stop laughing.

Why is it when I wind up a watch, I start it and when I wind up a poem, I end it?

It's A Strange World We Live In

What's the point in being pessimistic? – it doesn't work anyway.
Why do bills travel through the post at twice the speed of cheques?
Why do people who know the least shout the loudest?
What happens if you are scared half-to-death twice?
Why do writers write but fingers don't fing?
Why use a big word when a diminutive one will do?
Why is the third hand on your watch called the second hand?
If two mouses are mice, and two louses lice, why aren't two houses hice?
Why does 'fat chance' and 'slim chance' mean the same?
Why is a carrot more orange than an orange?
What would a chair look like if your knees bent the other way?
Do married people live longer than single people or does it just
seem that way?
If a deaf person swears, does his mother wash his hands with soap?
Are you not frightened that doctors call what they do 'a practice'?
If a turtle doesn't have a shell, is it homeless or naked?
If the police arrest a group of mime artists, do they have the right
to remain silent?
When an agnostic dies, does he go to the 'Great Perhaps'?
Can atheists get insurance for Acts of God?
Why is the time of day with the slowest traffic called the rush hour?
How does skating on thin ice get you into hot water?
Tell a man there are 400 billion stars and he believes you; tell him
there is wet paint on a door and he has to touch it.
Why do we press harder on a remote control when we know the
battery is dead?
Doesn't expecting the unexpected make the unexpected become
the expected?
If all the world is a stage, where does the audience sit?
If you are cross-eyed and have dyslexia, can you read all right?

Pearls Of Wisdom To Improve
The Art Of The Quick Retort

42.7% of all statistics are made up on the spot.

99% of accountants give the rest a bad name.

A closed mouth gathers no foot.

All generalisations are false, including this one.

Always remember: You're unique, just like everyone else.

Anything worth taking seriously is worth making fun of.

Artificial Intelligence usually beats real stupidity.

Assassins do it from behind.

Beauty is in the eye of the beer holder.

Beer: It's not just for breakfast anymore.

Boycott shampoo! Demand the REAL poo!

Chocolate: The OTHER major food group.

Corduroy pillows: They're making headlines!

Death is hereditary.

Double your drive space. Delete Windows!

Duct tape is like the force, it has a light side and a dark side and it holds the universe together.

Eagles may soar, but rabbits don't get sucked into jet engines.

Experience is something you don't get until just after you need it.

For Sale: Parachute. Only used once, never opened, small stain.

Friends help you move. Real friends help you move bodies.

Friends may come and go, but enemies tend to accumulate.

Generally speaking, you aren't learning much when your mouth is moving.

Genius does what it must, talent does what it can, and you had best do what you're told.

Give me ambiguity or give me something else.

Good judgment comes from bad experience and a lot of that comes from bad judgment.

Honk if you love peace and quiet.

Honk if you want to see my finger.

Monday is an awful way to spend 1/7th of your life.

My reality cheque just bounced!

If at first you don't succeed, skydiving is not for you.

If ignorance is bliss, you must be orgasmic.
If you think nobody cares if you're alive, try missing a couple of car payments.
Tax Office Motto: We've got what it takes to take what you've got.
It may be that your sole purpose in life is simply to serve as a warning to others.
It's lonely at the top, but you eat better.
Make it idiot proof and someone will make a better idiot.
Suicidal twin kills sister by mistake!
Oh Lord, give me patience, and GIVE IT TO ME NOW!!!

Some Wile Hard Questions

Daddy, why doesn't this magnet pick up this floppy disk?
Despite the cost of living, have you noticed how popular it remains?
Ever stop to think, and forget to start again?
How can fat people go skinny dipping?
How come Barbie is so popular if you have to buy her friends?
How do you tell when you run out of invisible ink?
How does Teflon stick to the pan?
How many roads must a man travel down before he admits he is lost?
How can a stupid person be a smart arse?
Have you ever imagined a world with no hypothetical situations?
If all is not lost, where is it?
If you tied buttered toast to the back of a cat and dropped it from a great height, which would land the right way up?
If you were in a vehicle travelling at the speed of light and turned off the headlights, what would happen?
Is life a sexually transmitted disease?
If you throw a cat out of a car window, does it become cat litter?
If corn oil comes from corn, where does baby oil come from?
If it is the tourist season, why can't we shoot them?
If you write a book about failure and it doesn't sell, are you a success?
If a parsley farmer does overtime, do they garnish his wages?
If carrots are so good for the eyes, why do you see so many dead rabbits on the road?

If flying is so safe, why do they call the airport the terminal?
If 'Q' is castrated, does it become 'O'?
If Superman could stop bullets with his chest, why did he duck when a gun was thrown at him?
If love is blind, why is lingerie so popular?
If God dropped acid, would he see people?
If one synchronized swimmer drowns, do the rest have to drown too?
If work is so terrific, how come they have to pay you to do it?
If you're born again, do you have two belly buttons?
If you choke a Smurf, what colour does it turn?
Isn't having a smoking section in a restaurant like having a peeing section in a swimming pool?
What was the best thing before sliced bread?
What do you do when you see an endangered animal that eats only endangered plants?
What's another word for thesaurus?
What's the speed of dark?
What is a free gift? Aren't all gifts free?
Whose bright idea was it to put an 's' in lisp?

Marriage Is...

Marriage is a matter of give and take, but so far I haven't been able to find anybody who'll take what I have to give.
Marriage is a mutual relationship if both parties know when to be mute.
Marriage is a rest period between romances.
Marriage is a three-ring circus: engagement ring, wedding ring, and suffering.
Marriage is a trip between Niagara Falls and Reno.
Marriage is bliss. Ignorance is bliss. Ergo...
Marriage is like a hot bath. Once you get used to it, it's not so hot.
Marriage is one of the chief causes of divorce.
Love may be blind but marriage is a real eye-opener.

Dodgy Advice

Hard work has a future payoff. Laziness pays off now.

If at first you don't succeed, destroy all evidence that you tried.

If at first you don't succeed, blame someone else and seek counselling.

Never ask a barber if he thinks you need a haircut.

Never do card tricks for the group you play poker with.

Never mess up an apology with an excuse.

Never miss a good chance to shut up.

Never test the depth of the water with both feet.

Never underestimate the power of stupid people in large groups.

Never wrestle with a pig: You both get all dirty and the pig likes it.

Plan to be spontaneous – tomorrow.

Save the whales: Collect the whole set.

Save your breath: You'll need it to blow up your girlfriend!

If you must choose between two evils, pick the one you've never tried before.

If you can't convince them, confuse them.

If you tell the truth, you don't have to remember anything.

Support bacteria, they're the only culture some people have.

Be nice to your kids. They'll choose your nursing home.

Smile, it's the second best thing you can do with your lips.

It's always darkest before dawn. So if you're going to steal the neighbour's newspaper, that's the time to do it.

Learn from your parents' mistakes: Use birth control.

Borrow money from pessimists, they don't expect it back.

Always try to be modest, and be proud of it!

Don't sweat the petty things, and don't pet the sweaty things.

Don't be irreplaceable; if you can't be replaced, you can't be promoted.

Beware of the toes you step on today. They could be attached to the ass you may have to kiss tomorrow.

Before you criticise someone, you should walk a mile in their shoes. That way, when you criticise them, you're a mile away and you have their shoes.

Wear short sleeves! Support your right to bare arms!

When you don't know what you are doing, do it neatly.

Ain't That The Truth!

A fool and his money are soon partying.
Many people quit looking for work when they find a job.
No-one is listening until you make a mistake.
By the time you can make ends meet, they move the ends.
On the other hand, you have different fingers.
Everything should be made as simple as possible, but no simpler.
For every action there is an equal and opposite criticism.
Half the people you know are below average.
He who smiles in a crisis has found someone to blame.
Sex is like air: it's not important unless you aren't getting any.
Some days you're the fly, some days you're the windscreen.
Some drink at the fountain of knowledge; others just gargle.
Some people are only alive because it is illegal to shoot them.
Success always occurs in private and failure in full view.
The colder the x-ray table, the more of your body is required on it.
The hardness of butter is directly proportional to the softness of the bread.
The more you complain, the longer God makes you live.
The only substitute for good manners is fast reflexes.
The problem with the gene pool is that there is no lifeguard.
The quickest way to double your money is to fold it in half and put it
back in your pocket.
The severity of the itch is inversely proportional to the ability to reach it.
The shortest distance between two points is under construction.
The sooner you fall behind, the more time you'll have to catch up.
The more trivial your research, the more people will read it and agree.
The more vital your research, the less people will understand it.
The nice thing about standards is that there are so many of them
to choose from.
The number of people watching you is proportional to the stupidity
of your action.
There is always one more imbecile than you counted on.
The universe is a figment of its own imagination.
There's no future in time travel.
Things are more like they are now than they ever were before.
Time is the best teacher; unfortunately it kills all of its students.

Time is what keeps everything from happening at once.
Time may be a great healer, but it's a lousy beautician.
Timing has an awful lot to do with the outcome of a rain dance.
To steal ideas from one person is plagiarism; to steal from many
is research.
To succeed in politics, it is often necessary to rise above your principles.
We were born naked, wet and hungry. Then things got worse.
A procrastinator's work is never done.
Some days you're the dog, some days you're the hydrant.
The only difference between a rut and a grave is the depth.
It's hard to make a comeback when you haven't been anywhere.
He who laughs last thinks slowest.
Nothing is fool-proof to a sufficiently talented fool.
The most precious thing we have is life. Yet it has absolutely no
trade-in value.
You can do more with a kind word and a gun than with just a kind word.
If everything seems to be going well, you have obviously
overlooked something.

Why...?

Why do psychics have to ask you for your name?
Why is abbreviation such a long word?
Why is lemon juice made with artificial flavour and washing-up liquid
made with real lemons?
Why do sheep not shrink in the rain?
Why isn't there a special name for the tops of your feet?
Why is it necessary to nail down the lid of a coffin?
Why is it that rain drops and snow falls?
Why don't we ever see the headline 'Psychic Wins Lottery'?
Why isn't there a mouse-flavoured cat food?
Why doesn't glue stick to the inside of the bottle?
Why does the sun lighten your hair and darken your skin?
Why is there an expiry date on cartons of sour cream?
Why do they sterilize the needles for a lethal injection?

Why do they call it a television set when there is only one of them?
Why isn't phonetic spelled the way it sounds?
Why put off till tomorrow what you can put off till the day after?

Mars And Venus

Women who seek to be equal to men lack ambition.
Women like silent men: they think they're listening.
Hell hath no fury like the lawyer of a woman scorned.
Many a wife thinks her husband is the world's greatest lover. But she can never catch him at it.
All men are idiots, and my wife married their king.
Get a new car for your spouse: it'll be a great trade!
Give a man a fish and he will eat for a day. Teach him how to fish, and he will sit in a boat and drink beer all day.
Give a man a free hand and he'll run it all over you.
The sex was so good that even the neighbours had a cigarette.
There are two theories to arguing with women. Neither one works.
A woman will dress up to go shopping, water the plants, empty the rubbish, answer the phone, read a book, and get the mail. A man will dress up for weddings and funerals.
Men wake up as good-looking as they were when they went to bed but women somehow deteriorate during the night.
Women love cats. Men say they love cats, but when women aren't looking, men kick cats.
A woman knows all about her children. She knows about their dentist appointments and romances, best friends, favourite foods, secret fears and hopes and dreams. A man is vaguely aware of some short people living in the house.
Men are from earth. Women are from earth. Deal with it.

Inventive Insults

100,000 sperm and you were the fastest?

Any similarity between you and a human is purely coincidental!

Anyone who told you to be yourself couldn't have given you worse advice.

Are your parents siblings?

As an outsider, what do you think of the human race?

Auntie Em, hate you, hate Kansas, taking the dog. Dorothy.

Did your parents ever ask you to run away from home?

Don't let you mind wander – it's far too small to be let out on its own.

Do you ever wonder what life would be like if you'd had enough oxygen at birth?

Do you want people to accept you as you are, or do you want them to like you?

Don't you have a terribly empty feeling – in your skull?

Do you still love nature, despite what it did to you?

Don't you need a licence to be that ugly?

Every girl has the right to be ugly, but you abused the privilege!

Forget the health food. You need all the preservatives you can get.

Have you considered suing your brains for non-support?

He does the work of three men: Larry, Moe and Curly.

He's not stupid; he's possessed by a retarded ghost.

I'd like to see things from your point of view but I can't seem to get my head that far up my ass.

I bet your brain feels as good as new, seeing that you've never used it.

I could make a monkey out of you, but why should I take all the credit?

I don't consider you a vulture. I consider you something a vulture would eat.

I don't know what makes you so stupid, but it really works!

I don't think you are a fool. But then, what's MY opinion against thousands of others?

I hear the only place you're ever invited is outside.

I heard you got a brain transplant and the brain rejected you!

I know you are nobody's fool but maybe someone will adopt you.

I'd like to leave you with one thought... but I'm not sure you have anywhere to put it!

I'll never forget the first time we met – although I'll keep trying.

I'm busy now. Can I ignore you some other time?

I've seen people like you before, but I had to pay admission!

If I ever need a brain transplant, I'd choose yours because I'd want a brain that had never been used.

If we were to kill everybody who hates you, it wouldn't be murder; it would be genocide!

If you stand close enough to him, you can hear the ocean.

If your brain were chocolate, it wouldn't fill an M&M.

So, a thought crossed your mind? Must have been a long and lonely journey.

There is no vaccine against stupidity.

You are depriving some poor village of its idiot.

You're as useful as a grave robber in a crematorium.

You're as much use as an ashtray on a motorbike.

You're as useless as a carpet fitter's ladder.

You're as useful as a one-armed trapeze artist with an itchy arse.

You're as much use as a one-legged cat trying to bury a turd on a frozen lake.

You're as much use as mudguards on a tortoise.

You're as much use as a one-legged man at an arse-kicking competition.

You're as much use as Captain Hook at a gynaecologists' convention.

You're as much use as a trapdoor on a lifeboat.

Your gene pool could use a little chlorine.

You're that unlucky, if you were reincarnated you would come back as yourself.

Scorchio!

One tequila, two tequila, three tequila, floor.

Veni, vidi, velcro: I came, I saw, I stuck around.

Veni, vidi, Pesci: I came, I saw, I blew away that damn wiseguy.

Domino vobiscum: the pizza's here.

All About Me

I am not a vegetarian because I love animals. I am a vegetarian because I hate plants.

I am a nobody, nobody is perfect, therefore I am perfect.

I couldn't repair your brakes, so I made your horn louder.

I nearly had a physic girlfriend once, but she left me before we met.

I don't suffer from insanity. I enjoy every minute of it.

I feel like I'm diagonally parked in a parallel universe.

I get enough exercise just pushing my luck.

I just got lost in thought. It was unfamiliar territory.

I like kids, but I don't think I could eat a whole one.

I live in my own little world, but it's OK, they know me here.

I need someone really bad. Are you really bad?

I doubt, therefore I might be.

I poured Spot remover on my dog. Now he's gone.

I took an IQ test and the results were negative.

I tried sniffing Coke once, but the ice cubes got stuck in my nose.

I used to be indecisive. Now I'm not sure.

I used to have a handle on life, and then it broke.

I used up all my sick days, so I'm calling in dead.

I used to have an open mind but my brains kept falling out.

I won't rise to the occasion, but I'll slide over to it.

I wouldn't be caught dead with a necrophiliac.

I'm not a complete idiot, some parts are missing!

I'm writing a book. I've got the page numbers done.

I'm as confused as a baby in a topless bar.

I'm an apathetic sociopath – I'd kill you if I cared.

As I said before, I never repeat myself.

My favourite mythical creature? The honest politician.

My mind is like a steel trap, rusty and illegal in 37 countries.

I don't have a solution but I admire the problem.

I drive way too fast to worry about cholesterol.

Don't piss me off! I'm running out of places to hide the bodies.

I intend to live forever – so far, so good.

Take my advice; I don't use it anyway.

When I'm finally holding all the cards, why does everyone decide to play chess?

When I'm not in my right mind, my left mind gets pretty crowded.

If God wanted me to touch my toes, he would have put them on my knees.

If things get any worse, I'll have to ask you to stop helping me.

Where there's a will, I want to be in it.

Daft Definitions

A conclusion is the place where you got tired of thinking.

A diplomat is someone who can tell you to go to hell in such a way that you will look forward to the trip.

A clean desk is a sign of a cluttered desk drawer.

A clear conscience is usually the sign of a bad memory.

A babysitter is a teenager acting like an adult while the adults are out acting like teenagers.

A banker is someone who lends you an umbrella when the sun is shining and who asks for it back when it starts to rain.

A bargain is something you cannot use at a price you cannot resist.

A budget is just a method of worrying *before* you spend money, as well as afterward.

A bus is a vehicle that runs twice as fast when you are after it as when you are in it.

A camel is a horse designed by a committee.

Atheism is a non-prophet organisation.

A celebrity is someone who works hard all his life to become known and then wears dark glasses to avoid being recognised.

A politician is someone who gets money from the rich and votes from the poor to protect them from each other.

A torch: A case for holding dead batteries.

Black holes are where God divided by zero.

Consciousness: That annoying time between naps.

Diplomacy is the art of saying good doggie while looking for a bigger stick.

Laughing stock: Cattle with a sense of humour.

Depression is merely anger without enthusiasm.

Heart attacks: God's revenge for eating his animal friends.

Impotence: Nature's way of saying 'no hard feelings'.
Lottery: A tax on people who are bad at maths.
Pride is what we have. Vanity is what others have.
Puritanism: The haunting fear that someone, somewhere may be happy.
Quantum mechanics: The dreams stuff is made of.
Reality is a crutch for people who can't handle drugs.
Dancing is a perpendicular expression of a horizontal desire.
The shin: A device for finding furniture in the dark.

Now We're Getting Philosophical

When you're going up the stairs and you take a step, kick the other leg up high behind you to keep people from following too close.

I have to laugh when I think of the first cigar, because it was probably just a bunch of rolled-up tobacco leaves.

If dogs ever take over the world, and they choose a king, I hope they don't just go by size, because I bet there are some Chihuahuas with some good ideas.

We tend to scoff at the beliefs of the ancient civilisations. But we can't scoff at them personally, to their faces, and this is what annoys me.

To me, clowns aren't funny. In fact, they're kind of scary. I've wondered where this started and I think it goes back to the time I went to the circus and a clown killed my best friend.

I think it's better not take a dog on the Space Shuttle, because if he sticks his head out when you're coming home, his face might burn up.

He doesn't know the meaning of the word 'fear' – but then again he doesn't know the meaning of most words.

It takes a big man to cry, but it takes an even bigger man to laugh at that man.

My grandfather always thought laughter was the best medicine, which is why several of his family died of tuberculosis.

To me, boxing is like a ballet, except there's no music, no choreography, and the dancers hit each other.

How long a minute is depends on what side of the bathroom door you're on.

I don't understand people who say life is a mystery. What is it they want to know?

Snowmen fall from Heaven unassembled.

The only perfect science is hindsight.

Leftists are among the first to speak of their rights.

Even crime wouldn't pay if the government ran it.

Kids in the back seat cause accidents; accidents in the back seat cause kids.

Anything worth fighting for is worth fighting dirty for.

Indecision is the key to flexibility.

All things being equal, fat people use more soap.

Raising teenagers is like nailing jelly to a tree.

Families are like fudge, mostly sweet, with a few nuts.

Growing old is mandatory; growing up is optional.

Wisdom comes with age, but sometimes age comes alone.

Clones are people two.

Ambition is a poor excuse for not having enough sense to be lazy.

24 hours in a day... 24 beers in a box... coincidence?

Reread carefully to make sure you don't out a word.

One nice thing about egotists: They don't talk about other people.

To be intoxicated is to feel sophisticated but not be able to say it.

Procrastination is the art of keeping up with yesterday.

Madness takes its toll. Please have exact change.

What has four legs and an arm? A happy pit bull.

I wonder if angels believe in ghosts.

The face of a child can say it all, especially the mouth part of the face.

Fond Memories

The memories of my family outings are still a source of strength to me. I remember we'd all pile into the car – I forget what kind of car it was – and drive and drive. I'm not sure where we'd go, but I think there were some trees there. The smell of something was strong in the air as we played whatever sport we played. I remember a bigger, older guy we called 'Da'. We'd eat some stuff, or not, and then I think we went home. I guess some things never leave you.

You Know You're Getting Old When...

Age is a very high price to pay for maturity.
You finally get your head together, now your body is falling apart.
Your wild oats have turned to prunes and All Bran.
You don't remember being absent-minded.
The older you get, the better you realise you were.
The only time the world beats a path to your door is if you're
in the bathroom.
Everything hurts, and what doesn't hurt doesn't work.
You feel like the morning after and you haven't been anywhere.
A dripping faucet causes an uncontrollable bladder urge.
Your mind makes contracts your body can't keep.
You look forward to a dull evening.
Your underwear starts creeping up on you – and you enjoy it.
You don't do drugs anymore because you can get the same effect just
by standing up really fast.
You light the candles on your birthday cake and a group of campers
form a circle and start singing *Kumbaya.*
Your back goes out more than you do.
Someone compliments you on your layered look – and you are
wearing a bikini.
Your insurance company has started sending you their free calendars –
a month at a time.
One of the throw pillows on your bed is a hot-water bottle.
It takes a couple of tries to get over a speed ramp.
You're asleep, but others think you are dead.
You can live without sex but not your glasses.
You have a party and the neighbours don't even realise it.
You find your self singing along with elevator music.
Your ears have more hair than your head.
You fall down, you wonder what else you can do while you're down there.
You get the same sensation from a rocking chair that you once got
from a roller coaster.
You choose your cereal for the fibre, not the joy.
You know all the answers, but nobody bothers to ask you the questions.

Women's One-Liners

I'm not your type. I'm not inflatable.
A hard-on does not count as personal growth.
This isn't an office. It's Hell with fluorescent lighting.
Do I look like a 'people person' to you?
I pretend to work. They pretend to pay me.
If I throw a stick, will you leave?
If I want to hear the patter of little feet, I'll put shoes on my cat.
Did the aliens forget to remove your anal probe?
See no evil, hear no evil, and date no evil.
Sarcasm is just one more service we offer.
Whatever kind of look you were going for, you missed.
I am doing my best to imagine you with a personality.
Not all men are annoying. Some are dead.
Too many freaks, not enough circuses.
And which dwarf are you?
How do I set a laser printer to stun?
It's not the size that counts, it's the... umm, actually, it *is* the size.

Unpublished Children's Books

You Were an Accident
Strangers Have the Best Candy
The Little Sissy Who Snitched
Some Kittens Can Fly
Getting More Chocolate on Your Face
Where Would You Like to be Buried?
Katy Was So Bad, Her Mom Stopped Loving Her
All Dogs Go to Hell
The Kids' Guide to Hitchhiking
When Mommy and Daddy Don't Know the Answer, They Say God Did It
Garfield Gets Feline Leukaemia
What is That Dog Doing to That Other Dog?
Why Can't Mr Fork and Mrs Socket be Friends?

Daddy Drinks Because You Cry
You Are Different and That's Bad
Pop Goes the Hamster and Other Great Microwave Games
The Hardy Boys, the Barbie Twins, and the Vice Squad
The Tickling Babysitter
Barney Meets the Taxidermist
The Tellytubbies and the High-Voltage Fence
The Boy Who Died From Eating All His Vegetables
Start a Business Empire With the Change From Your Mammy's Purse
The Pop-up Book of Human Anatomy
Things Rich Kids Have, But You Never Will
The Care Bears Maul Some Campers and are Shot Dead
How to Become the Dominant Military Power in Your School
Controlling the Playground: Respect Through Fear
Barney: The Prison Years

The Four Stages Of Life

1) You believe in Santa Claus.
2) You don't believe in Santa Claus.
3) You are Santa Claus.
4) You look like Santa Claus.

Five Stages Of Being Drunk

Stage 1: SMART
This is when you suddenly become an expert on every subject in the known Universe. You know you know everything and want to pass on your knowledge to anyone who will listen. At this stage, you are always RIGHT. And of course the person you are talking to is very WRONG. This makes for an interesting argument when both parties are SMART.

Stage 2: GOOD-LOOKING
This is when you realise that you are the BEST-LOOKING person in the entire bar and that people fancy you. You can go up to a perfect

stranger, knowing they fancy you and really want to talk to you. Bear in mind that you are still SMART, so you can talk to this person about any subject under the sun.

Stage 3: RICH
This is when you suddenly become the richest person in the world. You can buy drinks for the entire bar because you have an armoured truck full of money parked outside. You can also make bets at this stage, because of course you are still SMART, so naturally you win all your bets. It doesn't matter how much you bet because you are RICH. You will also buy drinks for everyone that you fancy, because you are still the BEST-LOOKING person in the world.

Stage 4: BULLETPROOF
You are now ready to pick fights with anyone and everyone, especially those with whom you have been betting or arguing. This is because nothing can hurt you. At this point, you can also go up to the partners of the people whom you fancy and challenge them to a battle of wits or money. You have no fear of losing this battle because you are SMART, you are RICH and, hell, you're BETTER LOOKING than they are anyway

Stage 5: INVISIBLE
This is the Final Stage of Drunkenness. At this point, you can do anything because NO ONE CAN SEE YOU. You dance on a table to impress the people whom you fancy because the rest of the people in the room cannot see you. You are also invisible to the person who wants to fight you. You can walk through the street singing at the top of your lungs because no-one can see or hear you, and, because you're still SMART, you know all the words.

Cultural Differences Explained

Aussies: Believe you should look out for your mates.

Brits: Believe that you should look out for those people who belong to your club.

Americans: Believe that people should look out for, and take care of, themselves.

Canadians: Believe that that's the government's job.

Derry Wans: A mate is a mucker and a mucker is someone you drink with, so drink with everyone.

Aussies: Dislike being mistaken for Brits when abroad.

Canadians: Are rather indignant about being mistaken for Americans when abroad.

Americans: Encourage being mistaken for Canadians when abroad.

Brits: Can't possibly be mistaken for anyone else when abroad.

Derry Wans: Is Buncrana abroad?

Americans: Spend most of their lives glued to the goggle box.

Canadians: Don't, but only because they can't get more American channels.

Aussies: Export all their crappy programs, which no-one there watches, to Britain where everybody loves them.

Brits: Pay a licence just so they can watch five channels.

Derry Wans: What's a licence?

Americans: Love to watch sports on the television.

Brits: Love to watch sports in stadiums so they can fight with other fans.

Canadians: Prefer to actually engage in sports rather than watch them.

Aussies: Love to get drunk and that is the national sport.

Derry Wans: Can do the lot as long as it involves greyhounds.

Americans:	Will slabber on incessantly about football, baseball and basketball.
Brits:	Will slabber on incessantly about cricket, soccer and rugby.
Canadians:	Will slabber on incessantly about hockey, hockey, hockey, and how they beat the Americans twice playing baseball.
Aussies:	Will slabber on incessantly about how they beat the Brits in every sport they played them in.
Derry Wans:	Just slabber.

Americans:	Spell words differently, but still call it 'English'.
Brits:	Pronounce their words differently, but still call it 'English'.
Canadians:	Spell like the Brits, pronounce like Americans.
Aussies:	Say 'G'day, mate,' and only talk about barbies and prawns.
Derry Wans:	Ken sae wat wae wunt, innytim, innywear, dae innywan.

Brits:	Shop at home and have goods imported because they live on an island.
Aussies:	Shop at home and have goods imported because they live on an island.
Americans:	Cross the southern border for cheap shopping, petrol and drink in a backward country.
Canadians:	Cross the southern border for cheap shopping, petrol and drink in a backward country.
Derry Wans:	Cross the border for cheap shopping, petrol and fags in a more advanced country.

Aussies:	Are extremely patriotic to their beer.
Americans:	Are flag-waving, anthem-singing, and obsessively patriotic to the point of blindness.
Canadians:	Can't agree on the words to their anthem, when they can be bothered to sing them.

Brits: Do not sing at all but prefer a large brass band to perform the anthem.

Derry Wans: 'Soldiers are wee.'

Americans: Drink weak, piss-tasting beer.

Canadians: Drink strong, piss-tasting beer.

Brits: Drink warm, beery-tasting piss.

Aussies: Drink anything with alcohol in it.

Derry Wans: Drink.

Brits: Are justifiably proud of the accomplishments of their past citizens.

Americans: Are justifiably proud of the accomplishments of their present citizens.

Canadians: Prattle on about how some of those great Americans were once Canadian.

Aussies: Spoof on about how some of their past citizens were once outlaw-Irish but none of that really matters after several beers.

Derry Wans: Can slag each other but nobody outside of here has the right to slag us.

Americans: Seem to think that poverty and failure are morally suspect.

Canadians: Seem to believe that wealth and success are morally suspect.

Brits: Seem to believe that wealth, poverty, success and failure are inherited things.

Aussies: Seem to think that none of this matters after several beers.

Derry Wans: We share everything, although it is easy to share everything when you have nothing.

Canadians: Encourage immigrants to keep their old ways and avoid assimilation.

Americans: Encourage immigrants to assimilate quickly and dump their old ways.

Brits:	Encourage immigrants to go to Canada or America.
Aussies:	Have you met my Dolly?
Derry Wans:	Little do the rest know but we invaded the world years ago.

Canadians:	Endure bitterly cold winters and are proud of it.
Brits:	Endure oppressively wet and dreary winters and are proud of it.
Americans:	Don't have to do either, and couldn't care less.
Aussies:	Don't understand what inclement weather means.
Derry Wans:	We have two types of weather; it's raining or it's about to rain.

Aussies:	Have produced comedians like Paul Hogan and Yahoo Serious.
Canadians:	Have produced many great comedians like John Candy, Martin Short, Jim Carey, Dan Akroyd, and many others.
Americans:	Think that these people are American!
Brits:	Have produced many great comedians, but Americans ignore them because they don't understand subtle humour.
Derry Wans:	Nobody takes our comedy serious.

Theatre And Drama

Over The Moon

The following monologue is an extract from my 2003 production, *Over the Moon*, which deals with contradictions in life and people.

Narrator: You want to be normal. You want to live a normal life, in a normal house, in a normal town, in a normal country, doing normal things with your normal family. I didn't make life abnormal so why should I suffer the abuse? I didn't make people angry or selfish or greedy or jealous. I didn't make them smoke, or drink too much or not eat the right food or gorge on the wrong food. Why should I be treated different? I didn't make the world strange or evil.

The world is a strange place and so is life. Life is full of paradoxes. These days you have taller buildings but shorter tempers. You want more. You spend more money but have less. You buy more but enjoy it less. You have bigger houses for smaller families. You have more conveniences but less free time. You have more degrees but less common sense. You have more knowledge but less judgement. You have more experts to deal with more problems created by experts in the first place.

Nowadays you spend too recklessly, laugh too little, drive too fast, get too angry, stay up too late, get up too tired, read too seldom, watch too much TV, and pray too seldom. You have multiplied your possessions and reduced your values. You talk too much and listen less, love too seldom, and are bored too quick. You've learned how to make a living, but not to have a life. I tell you what, you've added years to life, not life to the years.

You've been all the way to the moon and back, but have trouble crossing the street to meet the new neighbour. You've developed smart bombs to do stupid things. You've conquered outer space, but not inner space; You've done larger things, but not better things; you've cleaned up the air, but polluted the soul; you've split the atom, but not our prejudice; you write more, but learn less; plan more, but accomplish less. You've learned to rush, but not to wait. You have higher incomes; but lower morals; more food but less appetite; more acquaintances, but fewer friends; more effort but less success.

These are the times of tall men with short character, steep profits and shallow pockets. These should be the times of world peace, not global warfare. You have more leisure, but less fun; more kinds of food, but less nutrition. These are the days of two incomes, but more divorces; of fancier houses, but broken homes.

These are days of quick trips, disposable nappies, throwaway morality, one-night stands and pills that do everything from cheer, to quiet, to kill. It is a time when there is much in the shop window and plastic in the pocket. A time when corruption is the rule, not the exception. Indeed it's all true; mark my words, these are my days. These are the days when there are vicious attacks on pensioners and health workers, heroin on the estates, tax evasion and shady deals, fat cats lapping the cream, shirt factories closing, off-shore accounts and tightening purse strings, low pay for more hours, poverty etched on children's faces, families in turmoil and over the hill at thirty. These are the days that are crying out for heroes. Do you want a hero? There are no more heroes anymore; I am the only vestige for freedom. I am your hero! You'll never walk alone when I am at your side. Feed me. Isn't that right, Papa Joe?

Under Pressure

Over the years, I have been heavily involved in developing Theatre and Drama techniques in the classroom. Since 1997, in my professional capacity as an Arts Educator with the Verbal Arts Centre, I have worked with over 8,500 young people from the North West area and beyond. Many of these young people experience difficulties in their school, personal or social life. Some young people experience severe personal trauma, intensive behavioral and social problems, substance-abuse problems and feelings of exclusion and marginalisation.

The following two extracts are from a 2001 play, *Under Pressure*. I, with Gillian Kennedy and my other colleagues at the Verbal Arts Centre, worked intensively with a group of young teenagers and developed an original script that toured extensively throughout the North of Ireland as well as making a film of the play. The play deals with over twenty-five issues, and the central theme is why young people would choose suicide as an option. The Narrator of the play is Benny who lives his life at the edge and feels totally outside of the community and family. This is the opening scene and the audience gets a feeling about the character and the life he leads.

Act One: Scene One

Narrator: Do I hear you asking yourself, 'What's this all about?' But I'm sure that's not the language you're using. Well, friends, this is about life. To be more particular, it's about *my* life. So, where do I start? I know, let me introduce you to all the people who have the greatest influence on me as a person.

I have a problem. In fact, I have several problems. Most of the problems have little to do with me but more so other people. You see, other people give me problems. I am what you could call a hassle magnet. For example, I have a girlfriend called Emma. (*From her area, Emma waves*) She thinks I'm great but she puts too much pressure on me. By the way, I think she's great, especially in the sack department. And there is my gang, my muckers. (*The four boys wave as if being called*) And my family. (*They wave from their playing area*) And there's the fountain of my knowledge, the old school. (*Those in the school scene wave*) So you see, that's where it all comes from. I think the sociologists call it the 'socialisation process'. All the people who have the most influence on me as a person. (*Everyone waves*) I am so proud of them. And what a bunch of losers they are. Negative and annoying. Great role models indeed. Sure what do sociologists know? Some people think if you have an –ology you can say what you want and that's that. Well, you know what? I have an –ology, my own special –ology. It's called me-ology. It means I can say and do what I want and that's that. But then, not everybody sees life the way that I do.

Mother: My son is a very special boy.

Narrator: Yes, mother, indeed I am very special, so very special.

Teacher: We will give your son very special treatment indeed.

Narrator: And of course they did.

Emma: You know you are really special to me.

Narrator: Oh, I am. So you see, I am a very special lad. Oh so special. Do you know I am so special that I have to talk to a special doctor every week? The magistrate thought it would be a very special thing for me to do. *(Sprawls on a bench)* Well, Doctor, it all began at a very early age. You see, I was born. I never asked be born. I never asked to be part of that family. I never asked to be sent to that school. I never asked to go to court. I never asked to see you, Doctor. And I never asked for my life to be so messed up that I'd think I'd rather end it. Well, Doctor, what advice will you give me?

What secret tablet do you have that will take these feelings away? What would you advise? A rope? A big high bridge? A bag of colourful pills, maybe? A big cannon, maybe? Well, of course you're right, Doctor, I must think of all the people I will leave behind. Just the way they thought of me. Let me give you a sample of my life and you tell me whether it is worth saving.

Act One: Scene Eleven

In this second scene, and the closing scene to the play, the 'victim', for want of better term, is called Stanley and he experiences severe bullying because of his size and mannerisms. During the developmental stage of the play, bullying emerged as a major issue with young people, and this was reinforced during the workshops held with over 3,000 young people in every part of the region. Stanley (aka Moody Blue) has taken his life by throwing himself in front of a car, owned by his father but driven by car thieves who were unaware that he was contemplating such a tragic end to his young life. The play had a major impact wherever it played, and this was mainly due to relevance, amazing performances from the two casts and the need for theatre in education projects to be direct and pertinent.

Stanley: (*directly to the audience*) Well, there you are. Another story with a happy ending. Boy meets girl. Catholic meets Protestant. Black meets White. Good meets Bad. All the opposites attract. That's what makes the world go round. The faster it goes round, the more people's heads get dizzy and they want to get off. Get off and stay off. So I wonder if there is a point to it all? And if there is no point to it, why should we go through all of this. If the meaning of life is to live, how come I couldn't? People say that life is a mystery. They say that life is precious. They say: 'Don't waste your life, live it to the full.' There goes Moody Blue. Poor Moody Blue. Did you hear about Moody Blue? For the first time in my life, I was the focus of attention and not ridicule. If I lived in America, it would be so easy. I get a rifle, take it into school and then nobody would have messed me about. That would have been so easy. But I'm not in America. I am here. How do I deal with the hurt here? A kiss doesn't take the pain away. Genuine tears were cried at my funeral. People said they missed me already. But who'll care next week, next month, next year? When I was alive, no-one listened to me, no-one talked to me, no-one smiled with me. No-one was there for me when I needed to be held. No-one there for me. I lost hope. Did you ever feel the despair of losing hope? I stopped believing in myself. All I wanted was someone to hold me, hold me tight. Someone to share my tears and make me smile. Someone to love me. Love me until the pain stopped and the healing began.

It's Like This

This was a cross-border drama project developed by the Artemis Project at the Verbal Arts Centre and the Balor Theatre from Donegal in 2002. A group of 24 young people (14-16 years from Tyrone and Donegal) were involved in a project that looked at teenage relationships, bullying and disability discrimination. The play, using two casts, toured schools and theatres with an interactive workshop on the issues raised within the play. The play deals with the continuous bullying of Ali, a deaf teenager, who is one of the central characters in the play. The following three short monologues deal with the pressures of parenthood and living with a disability.

Act One: Scene Five

Maria's mother's monologue.

Maria's mother has an alcohol problem and experiences difficulties communicating with her only child, Maria. She walks on stage and finds a teddy bear on the floor. She lifts it and addresses the monologue almost to the toy.

Narrator: I remember the day I bought this. It was like yesterday. I was in the city at college. My first year in the big city, I was so excited. I loved it, the shops, the people, the buzz and of course the pubs. (*She thinks*) I remember it was raining the day I bought this for you, Maria. You weren't even born then. I was standing in a doorway of a toy shop. I was crying. But then I used to cry a lot then, especially then. Of course, I still cry nowadays but now I don't know why I'm crying anymore. Then, I had a reason. I suppose there's always a reason to cry. I was seventeen. I was young, free and single. The world was my oyster and I was a pearl. My whole life was opening up in front of me. It was so, so exciting. Then the crash came. As I left the doctor's surgery I could feel nothing, I was numbed, in shock. I will never forget that feeling. All I could see in front of me was my mother's look of disappointment and the sound of my father's silence. (*Mimics her mother's voice*) I knew this would happen. Didn't I tell you this would happen? No, you wouldn't listen to me. You never listen to me. (*Changes back to her own voice*) Oh, I listened all right! I listened to her right up until the day you were born. When you opened your eyes, you stole everyone's heart. You were so good at that, Maria. But then I am so good at blaming you for ruining my life. For making my life so boring. You took the excitement away from me, Maria. When the doctor told me I was pregnant, I said nothing until I stood looking in that toy shop window. You know, Maria, I passed that shop every day for a year and never once looked in the window. That day, I cried looking at the toys and the happiness in the faces of the children playing with them. I'm sure the salesman thought I was mad. I was still crying when I bought this. He asked if I was all right. I told him I was pregnant. He was the first person I told. The rising bump told everyone else. I could have been whatever I wanted to be. I had to be a mother, a wife, a drunkard. Life could have been so different if I wasn't so stupid. Maria, I do love you but it's just that I, well, you know. Maybe I should give this away, some child somewhere would love to cuddle up to this at night. Maria, I am so sorry that I was your mother, you deserved someone better. I'm so sorry. (*exit*)

Act One: Scene Eight

Ali is fifteen years old and is deaf. He has endured taunting, bullying and beatings as a result of being disabled and is constantly picked on by other boys. In this scene, Ali sits down on the platform alone and appears to have had a severe beating around his face. His eyes and face are swollen and reddened. His voice is tinged with sadness, anger and resentment.

Ali: *(to the audience)* Bullying is all about power. It's not just the marks you see on my face that hurt me. These marks will go away. The swelling will go down but the pain in my heart is the worse. It's not just the name calling, the nasty things they say about me, the threats, the beatings or the damage to my things. It's the fear. Ruthless and relentless fear. The fear that every time I leave the house something awful will happen to me. I know why they do it. They want to feel big, popular, look tough and put themselves in charge. They want me to feel scared. They want me to be lonely. As if my deafness is not lonely enough they want to isolate me more. There is nothing wrong with me. I am deaf. I am living with my deafness. I am proud to be who I am. They will not take my pride away. Nobody is born a bully. They learn it somewhere. What do I do? People say you must face your bully and confront him. What if the 'him' is a 'them'? What if I have to face a whole crowd of bullies? If I name and shame them, will it make my life worse or better? Tell someone, they say. I can tell but who will listen? I can stand at the top of the school building and yell at the top of my voice: 'Leave me alone!' Yes, I am scared. Yes, I fear for my life. If they don't take it, maybe I will. If someone doesn't do something soon, maybe I will.

Act One: Scene Nine

Angie is the central character and this is her final narrative on the play.

Angie: One morning the King of Siam was taking his breakfast on the battlements of his magnificent palace. He dropped a trickle of honey from his spoon and it fell onto the ground below. His Chief Advisor said that he would clean it up. The King said, 'Don't worry about it, it's not our problem.' A fly ate the honey. A toad ate the fly. A rat ate the toad. A cat ate the rat. A dog fought with the cat. The cat owner fought with the dog owner. The crowd in the market fought with each other. The palace guards fought with the crowd and then the army fought with each other. Brother fought brother. Father fought son, who fought brother. The civil war lasted ten bloody years. As the King stood on the battlements of his burning palace, he said to his Chief Advisor, 'It *was* our problem, wasn't it?'

What happened to Ali was everybody's problem and we chose to ignore it. How many more Alis are there? How many of you would turn your back and ignore it?

Aileach

This was perhaps the largest and most ambitious production I have been involved in. With over 140 singers, dancers and actors, the play told a mythological tale of druids, the coming of Christianity to Ireland and Celtic warriors. Ever since I was a child, I have been captivated with the Grianan of Aileach, a stone fort built just outside Derry at Burt in County Donegal. I played on her battlements, meandered through her tunnels and rolled effortlessly on her slopes. It is suggested that the fort may be at least 5,000 years old. With fellow producer Ivor Ferris of the Cumann Gaelach Chnoc na Ros and Assistant Director Gillian Kennedy, we offered this triumph of creative will over practical realism to an incautious audience in 1999. This scene recreates the meeting of the two druid priests as they try to 'suss' each other out.

Act One: Scene Six

Annan: I have heard Cliodna, Queen of Faery Island, sing and soothe
          the sick to sleep.
          I have seen three bright birds calm the ocean.
          I have tasted the sweet fruit from the Trees of Plenty when
          guarded by Dagda Mor, the Earth God.
          I have seen Lugh's spear of shining heat as it sliced through the
          wind and tamed the God of the angry sea.
          I have eaten at the table of Mannanan and worn his cloak
          of invisibility.
          I was there when Nuada, the first King of Tara, lost his hand
          fighting the Firbolg.
          I am wary of the invasion of these White Robes.
          Dagda. the fire beneath the cauldron
          Lord of Secret Knowledge.
          Fire in the belly that sustains life,
          Fire in the loins that continues life,
          Fire in eye that understands life,
          Be in us and be with us because
          We are Aileach,

We are Eireann,
We are Celts,
We will live forever.

Thunder roars as he kneels down with his staff high above his head. The sound of taunting clapping is heard from the ramparts.

Voice: How apt to see you on your knees.

Annan: Who goes there under the cover of darkness?

Voice: I was told you were a snivelling dog who spends his time hiding under the skirts of old women. They told me your enemies are many and they tell the truth.

Annan: Show yourself.

Voice: Get off your knees, Annan.

Annan: Show yourself.

Voice: My, my, how the mighty Annan, High Druid Priest of Aileach, squeals like a little old woman when he is scared.

Annan: I fear neither man, beast or spirit. How did you get past the sentries on guard?

Voice: A little sweep of my robes and they are cowering like you. It's difficult to get the right calibre of guard these days.

He emerges from the darkness. He is wearing a beautiful scarlet robe with brightly coloured designs. This is the first time that the two druid priests have met each other. After a number of rumours about their specific abilities, they are very wary of each other. Almost like two gunslingers, they eye each other up. They circle and attempt to stare out the other. Both are dressed in ceremonial robes of scarlet and crimson. They wear the crowned hats

depicting their seniority. They stand silently and stare intently at each other,
taking in every aspect of their personae.

Oisin: I have learned my magic from the breast of Mother Earth. The
          eagle has taught me words and the languages that come from
          across the wild oceans.

Annan: The salmon has taught me knowledge, the ability to understand
          these languages and to sage beyond human thought.

Oisin: The skin of the King Bull has given me dreams where I can
          see beyond the reaches of a thousand eyes.

Annan: The animal spirits of the boar, the horse and the serpent have
          given me the wisdom of Dagda. I have the fertility of a dozen
          thousand men.

Oisin: I foresaw the death of the Fianna.

Annan: I caused the death of the Fianna.

Oisin: I have walked through the lands of the Other World, drunk
          from the waters of magic, breathed the dragon's fire breath and
          put nine-score men to their maker with the flash of my sword.

Annan: I gorge on the flesh of defeat and wallow in the mire of
          the fallen.

Oisin: I curse your tribe and call famine to your lands. May the seven
          terriers of the Other World sit on the spool of your heart and
          bark at your soul case.

Annan: May the spears of battle take your heart and roast your eyes on
          a spit made from the burning flesh of five virgins.

Oisin: May the curse of curses in sorrow prostrate you now.

Annan: May the serpent snap off your head and make a week's work on your neck, chest and limbs.

Oisin: May the curse of the diseased crows descend on you and all your future generations.

Annan: May the red stone come from the froth of the dragon's spit, swallow your seed and devour your ancestors' spirits.

Silence, then they embrace each other.

Together: BROTHER! (They embrace again)

Annan: Oh, Brother Druid, how well you are versed in the art of damnation.

Oisin: *(bows)* And you, my Brother, you have learned well.

Annan: We Brothers must consort with each other to ensure that the mortals' battle never affects the Druidic bonds.

Oisin: That is for fodder and lambs.

Annan: Well, Brother, what must we do to avert such a possibility?

Oisin: We must survive.

Annan: Indeed we must. It is good to meet a true Brother of the Mother Earth. My days have been like a slow callous death with the mutterings of the madmen who cause me such misery.

Oisin: Tell me what I don't know. They make a second seem like an eternity.

Annan: What of your King? How is his wit?

Oisin: His wit! (*Laughs aloud*) He can't see beyond his groin. The eye of a pretty maiden, a flicker of a smile, the smell of a scented breast. And yours?

Annan: As thick as a boar's tusk. His knowledge is in his wife's head. He asks: (*mimics the King*) 'Dear Queen Morna, what time of day is it?' She tells him it's dark when it's light and light when it's dark. He follows her around like a pig at the trough. Pitiful and sad springs to mind. Oh, Brother, our land is changing. But we should have been born in days gone by,

Oisin: There was magic in the old times. We Druids were true walkers between the worlds. We knew of Tír na nÓg and made our presence felt there. We stood by the De Danann in their time of need. We carried their stories and fables.

Annan: It is so true, Colleague. In the trances, we have learned our trade. The knowledge of the Other World will die at the hands of the Christians. We must wrap ourselves in the symbols of our belief. These impostors must be banished to the precipice of despair and abandoned to fear and ridicule.

Oisin: Manys a winter's night I have heard the old sages call out as they lay on their backs under the bull skin. I have heard their voices cut through the darkness and forewarn of this time. The Seanachie's stories warn us of the end. Our rituals will be swallowed by new words. What can we do to avert this?

Annan: We must instil the fear of the Other World.

Oisin: Of demons and dragons?

Annan: Of pookas and goblins?

Oisin: Of Morrigan?

Annan: Of Morrigan?

Together: Morrigan!

Oisin: We must conspire to make sure that, regardless of victory, the true enemy are the White Robes and that the swords of destiny are sharpened and slice true.

Annan: We have caught one here today.

Oisin: Then you must interrogate him until he denounces his faith in front of the many so even the few will have doubts. You must question him and find out more about this Judean preacher.

Annan: That was my second intention. My first was to run him through. The King believes that he will make a good plaything to distract us all from the conflict with Sobarce.

Oisin: Don't you worry about Sobarce. He is as superstitious as they come. He won't cross a river if there are salmon to be seen. Won't ride his horses if a raven is watching him. He won't eat if there is a white-haired boy serving him. All the products of my healthy imagination. So when I say don't worry, don't you concern yourself with Sobarce. He will do exactly as I say.

Annan: And what will you tell him?

Oisin: I will tell him to lay siege to the kingdom of Aileach and to seize it as his own. What a ring on his finger that would be! I am always astounded by the view from those ramparts. The benefits of winning this fort far outweigh the disadvantages. Of course you will be well provided for. You shall be our resident Druid and we will turn this fort into a seat of learning for Druids and Bards. It will be a centre for music and dance. It will attract Druids from every kingdom in this world. It will be a sacred place.

Annan: And what must I do?

Oisin: You must do as I say. Sobarce's army lies a sunrise march from here. It is his intention to ask Eoghan for Saoirse's hand in marriage. For his idiot son Lorcan. It is your responsibility to ensure that she agrees. Prince Lorcan is a fool. He has bread for brains. You will ensure that Saoirse will accept the offer of handfasting. That way, we can avoid the fighting and this will ensure that we have our plans in motion. As soon as the handfasting is in place, we can make our move to capture the kingdom without a drop of blood being spilt. Especially our blood.

Annan: Be careful, because, like the wild wolf, Saoirse will bark at her own shadow.

Oisin: Remember, Annan, a closed mouth is a wise head.

Annan: I will do what I can do.

Oisin: Of course you must. I'll be on my way now so by morning light we will meet again. (*They embrace*) To the future, Brother.

Annan: To the future.

They both exit.

Act One: Scene Eight

The children gather around the story chair for words of wisdom from Annan, the druid priest. He enters to the noisy anticipation of the children. He moves through the crowd of children and they excitedly follow him. As he sits on the story chair, they gather around his feet.

1st Child: Annan, where does the moon come from?

2nd Child: And where does the sun come from?

3rd Child: And the wind?

Annan: Children, children, please, one question at a time.

1st Child: And the water in the river?

Annan: Be patient! Patience is a virtue.

2nd Child: What is a virtue?

Annan: My son, if I get to know you as I know your father, you will
              never know the meaning of the word. But anyway, listen.

3rd Child: Annan will tell us a story.

Annan: From the olden days, when the land was made from the
              foam of the sea and force of the wind, there is a story.

3rd Child: See, I told you Annan will tell us a story!

Annan: Be quiet. Now sit up straight and listen because it is a story
              about the history of our land. Once upon a time, there was
              no time and there were no Gods, and no man or animal
              walked the surface of the land. But there was the sea, and
              where the sea met the land, there was foam and from the
              foam, a giant mare was made. The mare was Eiocha. On
              the land, a magic tree grew. The tree was a strong and
              sturdy oak tree. And on this mighty oak tree grew a plant
              with magic berries. The tears of the crashing foam formed
              the oak and berries. To sustain life, Eiocha ate the magic
              berries and the seeds grew within her. Eiocha grew heavy
              with child and gave birth to the God Cernunnos. So great
              were her childbirth pains that she tore bark from the oak
              tree and threw it in the sea. The bark was transformed in

the foam of the sea and became giants of the deep. Knowing her work was finished on land, Eiocha slipped quietly into the sea. Cernunnos grew big and strong and he coupled with the giants from the deep and they created the Godess Epona. The God Cernunnos and the Godess Epona became bored, as they had no-one to command or worship them. So they took wood from the giant oak tree and made the first man and woman. From the leaves and branches they fashioned animals. They made the hound, the boar and the hare. Then they made the birds of the sky, the raven, the eagle and the owl. Cernunnos commanded the oak tree to grow higher and further and it became a home to the animals, birds and their children. Epona took a branch from the tree and made a bow and arrows, then she made clubs and spears. She made thunderbolts from the echoes in the trunk of the oak. She took a limb from the tree and she made a harp. She made the strings from the gentle silver rains that fell on the land. She made music from the breeze and wind. The animals and the birds would gather in the bough of the tree and listen to the music that came from the magic harp. Everyone would bathe in the tranquillity of the peace and music. The Giants of the deep were jealous of the music and the peace. They met and plotted to invade the land. They decided they would cover it with foam. But in the depths of the ocean, the great Godess Eiocha heard what the Giants were planning. Eiocha told the God Cernunnos and the Godess Epona that the Giants were on their way so everyone on land hid in the bough of the sacred oak tree. They waited until the right moment and they attacked the Giants using the bows and arrows, clubs and spears made by Epona. Using a thousand thunderbolts, they attacked the Giants as they walked from the sea across the land. The Gods were swift in their attack and drove most of the Giants back into the sea. Some of the Giants escaped and they fled to the edge of the world and plotted revenge. They called themselves the Fomor. From the God Cernunnos and the Godess Epona came our mighty people, the Celts. From the fiery pieces of the Upperworld and the foamy depths of the Underworld came new Gods. The God Belenus and his sister Danu sprang from the thunderbolts and the God Lir came from the smashing of the foam on the rocks. From Lir would come the mighty Manannan. From Danu would come the Dagda, Nuadha of the Silver Hand, the fearsome Morrigan and the gentle Brighid. So it came to pass that our ancestors ruled the lands as far as man could travel. We forged our culture from the land of our history. Next time, I will tell you the story of the Children of Danu and the Children of Lir.

All the Children:	Praise be to Annan
1st Child:	Will you tell us another story?
2nd Child:	Will you tell us about the monsters and ghouls?
3rd Child:	Will you tell us how the sea was made?
1st Child:	Will you tell us about the White Robes?
Annan:	Enough! You will hear another tale of our Celtic peoples when next the sun rises before the moon catches her. Now you must prepare the bread for the meal. Go, before I swipe each of you with my staff of knowledge. Now go!

Lights and all exit

So You Want To Write A Play?

Playwrights build a physical construction on stage using, mostly, the spoken word. You can move around this construction (*the writer's world*) but it doesn't exist. That is part of the deal between the writer and the audience. So how do we create this world and these unique situations using actors' voices to create the construction and above all, make it believable?

Michael Weller (British playwright) has his views:
I don't write, I listen. I listen and just take dictation from my characters. I am a terrible speller and I don't have a sense of prose but I am a great listener so I write what I hear.

Playwrights, therefore, can make us hear what we have never heard said in that way before. Not just any old words but the uniqueness of the characters, the way they say things and what they talk about.

So if you want to be a playwright, you learn to listen more than you talk.

The Subjects Of Plays

Noted South African writer Athol Fugard says:
Let me simplify it. Never an idea; never, never, never has an idea led to a play. Every inspiration, every seminal image for a play, has been something I've read in a newspaper, a story that was told to me, always an event external to myself.

Theatre is different from film. Most people's views are tarnished by the sophistication of television and the cinema. Theatre is a different medium that requires a different level of understanding, both from the writer as well as the audience. The skill of the writer is to make the experience worthwhile and alluring.

So where do you start?

Beginnings

So what comes first... the story? The characters? The place? What? In real terms it doesn't matter. They will each emerge as you require them. Don't panic. There are no set guidelines or golden rules.

Affecting the audience is why one writes a play in the first place. You don't write it for yourself, the actors or the director. Your role as the writer is to engage your audience. Unlike novels, plays don't have time to begin at the beginning. They usually begin at a point just before the primary conflict erupts within the story. This is called the 'point of attack'. This is usually the first thing the audience will see or hear as the play begins. As you are telling a story, you decide where in the history of the story the play commences. Plays need conflict to fuel their dramatic action. But remember that argument is not conflict. As in life, arguments tend to be circular and no-one tends to get anywhere. Dramatic conflict only happens when each character has a stake in the eventual outcome. Spread the development of the conflict throughout the piece or, in other words, don't fire all your shots at one time. Give your audience a roller coaster ride of emotions from start to finish. Make sure they expect the unexpected.

Characters

It doesn't matter whether you are writing the saddest tragedy or the funniest farce; take your characters seriously.

African-American writer Ntozake Shange says:
The character I'm creating is coming from me, has been nourished in whatever I am. And I would assume there are thousands of them there. And I want them to be as totally whoever they are; as young girls, old men, whoever. But they have got to know that they came out of female soil.

Taking your characters seriously also ensures that you are developing their complexities. In order for your characters to work on stage, they must always be believable. You must know how they would sound when they speak, what they look like, if they have any peculiar quirks or personality traits, know how they would behave in a certain situation etc, and it always helps to describe them in a character profile. As they are your creations, you must know their backgrounds, mental baggage and secrets. As you gave them life you must live with them long after the play is completed.

Sometimes what you leave out of the dialogue is important because it allows the audience to make assumptions about the character and the plot. This is called the 'subtext'. The subtext is the unwritten part of the play that the characters allow the audience to develop. This is an important part of the creative process.

What Is The Meaning Of The Play?

Plays always tend to be about something that matters, sometimes called the theme of the play. Themes come from personal values: the moral, social or political viewpoint of the writer. These views are expressed through the plot and the characters. Playwrights tend not to think about the theme of the play a lot, as it tends to be an integral part of the writing in the first place. What matters deeply to the writer will matter deeply to the audience.

What About Constructive Criticism?

This is by far the most difficult aspect of writing for the stage. Unlike a novel or short story, a poem or even a film, theatre is a live venue with a direct relationship with the stage and audience. Plays are mostly accessible and interactive and as such are the most public of the writer's actions. The writer, actors, director and audience are in the 'then-and-now'. As any writer is expected to be involved in the process, you must learn to accept the criticisms that are ascribed to your work. This is inevitable so you must groom yourself for the good and bad. Most playwrights nurture a special way of dealing with this inevitability. The secret is an old cowboy trick – 'head them off at the pass'. In other words, become your own worst critic. Develop the following skill: 'playwright-talking-to-self lines'. Ask yourself some of the following questions as you reread your draft work:

• Why are you telling me this?

• Where is this going?

- Did you say that before?

- Does this bore me?

- Is this a distraction?

- What is happening here?

- Do I believe this?

- How does this contribute to the overall piece?

- Is this character/scene/line really necessary?

So you want to write a play. Go for it!

Writing Exercises

Write about the biggest challenge you ever faced.

Describe, in detail, a favourite room of yours.

Fantasise about the 'big trip' that you want to take one day.

Recall an object that used to be important to you but has now disappeared.

Remember your most hated childhood food.

Recollect an article of clothing you once loved.

Remember a favourite song from a particular time in your life.

Describe your most romantic moment.

Write a recipe for a dish you love to cook and whom you would invite to share that meal with you.

Write about a time when you thought, 'What am I doing in this place?'

Relate how a recent event made you change your daily routine.

Write a tribute to your favourite writer.

Write a tribute to your favourite actor/actress.

Write a tribute to your favourite athlete.

Write a tribute to your favourite musician.

Write a tribute to your favourite popstar.

Write a letter to someone and say what you cannot say face-to-face.

Trace one particular colour that you've liked all your life. How has it influenced you?

Write about a dream you've had.

Write about the last the time you were really angry/sad/happy/ annoyed etc.

What has been your most memorable experience this year?

Relay an event from your childhood when you quarreled with one of your relatives.

Your best friend is blind. Take this person on a walk through the forest.

Write a poem of no less than five lines to include the following words: dogged, German, blue, beach and rain.

Recollect a childhood smell and why this one more than another.

Where would you like to be right now and why?

'Blue feels like broken hearts.' Why?

'Green feels like...'

'Black feels like...'

'Red feels like...'

What has been the most unusual experience you have had in your life?

If you had the choice, what period in history would you have lived in and why? ˙

Writing Comedy

Stand Up: Sit Down
Writing Comedy Is A Serious Business!

Writing comedy is regarded as the most difficult form of writing there is. That's because comedy is a personal thing – what makes one person laugh wouldn't raise a smile in someone else. Anyone can be funny occasionally, but to be consistently amusing can sometimes prove to be a very daunting task indeed. Yet if you have the ability and determination, it can be a most lucrative business. You will be contributing to a market which is constantly searching for fresh material and ever on the lookout for new writers. Also, there is a high burn rate for comedy writers and writing.

There are no hard and fast rules of comedy, and often the most original comedy is written by someone who breaks conventions. There is an insatiable market for scripts but there are not enough good writers to go round. Producers are desperately trying to find writers they can work with and commission with confidence.

Making The Effort

To be successful you have to take it seriously. It is a serious business and you are dealing with professional people. You have deadlines to meet so you must put the time and effort into it. How many times do we say we haven't got time? Everyone has the same number of hours in the day and we should all use them in the best possible way. Getting up an hour earlier is no great hardship. The birds have already been awake for several hours and it can be a time for quiet thoughts. Other people are at their most creative at the end of the day and prefer to work into the early hours. Some can work during their lunch break, others sit in the park. There is no set time for writing. It is up to you to use your time wisely and decide when your most creative period is.

Getting Started

Firstly, decide what kind of comedy it is going to be. Are you good at writing short pieces like sketches and quickies with strong and surprising tag lines? Does your strength lie in creating characters and situations? Maybe you prefer to write jokes for stand-up comedians? Perhaps you are better at developing visual ideas? Is it for children? Is it for the whole family or is it for an adult audience?

Every comedy sets its own tone – the important thing is for the writer to be consistent. That way, the audience knows what they are watching. What is plausible and funny to an audience in one show may seem stupid and inconceivable to the same audience in another show.

Never sit down in front of a blank sheet of paper. You'll never think of a thing. Carry a notebook around with you for at least a week before you start, and write down anything you see or hear that makes you smile. At the end of the week, pick the best three ideas from your notes, think of titles for them and throw all the other ideas in the wastepaper basket.

Write the titles at the top of three separate pages and then, working on all three sketches at the same time, write down everything you can think of connected to each of the three subjects. Just lists of words. Connections. Related subjects. When all three pages are full, pick the one with what looks like the best comic potential and put it on top of the pile. You are now going to start writing your first sketch.

1) Choose a setting. Avoid common setups like a doctor's surgery or 'Man Goes Into a Shop'. Think *original*. Only set the sketch in *one* location.

2) Don't make the sketch too long. Two minutes is a good length to start with.

3) If you're trying to sell your material to TV, don't put in anything too expensive like a helicopter. Most TV shows operate on a tight budget.

4) Three characters is more than enough for a two-minute sketch. Don't write for a cast of thousands.

5) Work *out loud*. Say the lines as you write them. You need to hear what the material sounds like.

6) Think about what is happening *visually* as well as the words. Describe the physical action in detail. What are the characters wearing? What do they look like? What are their names? (Don't just call your characters FIRST MAN, SECOND MAN. It will help to bring them to life in your mind.)

Brainstorming

Bounce comedy ideas off the people around you. Don't work in isolation. If you don't have a writing partner (which I highly recommend for this type of writing), throw funny ideas at your wife, boyfriend, brother, sister, teacher, mother, anyone who will listen. Even better would be to sit down in a room of around six people and brainstorm ideas in a group. Write down everything. Sift through it later. Hit shows like *Friends* and *Frasier* are sometimes written by as many as twelve people.

Where Do The Ideas Come From?

The standard question everyone asks is: 'Where do ideas come from?' The standard answer is: from everywhere and anywhere. Of course, it is not quite as simple as that. You must look around you, listen, observe and read. Life is full of comedy. Look for it.

You will find it everywhere – in bus queues, in supermarkets, in the street, at home, etc. Remember your notebook as ideas can strike at any time. Jot down conversations and situations you come across. Not the whole scene, just a few key words will do. These will help you later on when you come to develop the situation. Humour is based on human reactions to situations and circumstances. Ideas must be based on truth. You can exaggerate like *Red Dwarf,* be wild like *The Young Ones,* or outrageous like *Absolutely Fabulous*, but the initial idea must have a relationship to reality.

Another good source for ideas is the letters pages of newspapers and magazines. Read them thoroughly for snippets from real life which would make good stories. They can be a mine of inspiration. Take the basic idea and imagine what happens next.

Study the market: assess the performers and their styles; choose your targets; tailor your output to their needs. Then, and only then, do you stand a reasonable chance of having your work accepted. Watch as much TV as possible. Regardless of your writing ambitions, watch everything at every opportunity. It will increase your knowledge of sound plot construction, character relationships and good dialogue. If you see a comedy programme which doesn't make you laugh, ask yourself why not. Then rewrite it and see if it is any better.

If you're stuck, the best place to go looking for ideas for sketches is in reference books like, for example, *Halliwell's Film Guide*. A book like this lists thousands and thousands of movie titles and plot lines. Stick a pin in, read a description of the film and see if it sparks off any funny ideas. For example, your sketch could be a spoof of:

- A Western

- A space movie

- An historical romance

- A war film

- A Hollywood musical

- A documentary about snail farming in Gdansk.

Put A Spin On It

There are literally hundreds of thousands of potential starting points for a sketch. But once you find a subject, try not to approach it in an obvious way. For example, if you're writing a sketch about hairdressers, don't set it in a hairdressing salon, set it half-way up Mount Everest! (You may have seen a sketch like this in *Monty Python*.)

Working Backwards

Sketches really should have a strong finish, so always work *backwards*. Here's how to do it: Think of the punchline *first*. If you can't think of one after ten minutes, there probably isn't a good one there. If that happens, throw the whole idea into the bin and move onto your next sketch title.

Once you've got your funny ending, work out how to get there. Start by writing the line *immediately before* the funny end-line. When you've worked out the whole of the last ten seconds of the sketch, it's probably safe to go and think about the beginning.

Writing Exercises

To help you get going, here are a few tried and tested comedy formats for sketches:

- Escalation: Funny idea starts small and gets bigger and bigger, ending in chaos of ridiculous proportions.

- Lists: Sketches in which the bulk of the dialogue is a long list of funny items. The best example of this is 'Cheese Shop' in *Monty Python*.

- Mad Man, Sane Man: This format speaks for itself, but don't go for obvious settings.

- Dangerous Situations: For example, sketch set on flight deck of an aircraft.

- Funny Words: Sketches which use the sound of language itself to be funny. Example: use of the words 'blobby' or 'wobble' *(see Mr Bean)*.

- Old and New: Getting a laugh from putting something modern in an historical setting *(or vice versa)*. Example: Sir Walter Raleigh using a cigarette lighter.

- Big and Small: Getting humour from large differences in scale. Example: a mouse trying to make love to an elephant.

Try the following as exercises.

- Create five funny names for products and commercials to go with it or lines on funny names of products already out there, eg No-Nonsense Pantyhose; Hotpoint for a refrigerator, etc.

- Create two 'What-if' sketches. What if a book salesperson found himself in the camp of Attila the Hun, or a social worker was suddenly having lunch with Cleopatra? Or take a famous person and put him/her into a trivial domestic situation which nearly gets in the way of a famous discovery or invention or moment, eg Edison thinking he has the light bulb working only to have to deal with his mother wanting help rearranging the furniture.

- Write some dialogue for a comedy sketch involving a conservative middle-aged businesswoman and a punk-rock teen bicycle messenger trapped together in an elevator.

Edit Your Work

When you have finished writing your sketch remember: *it is only the first draft*. Go back and look at it again. Improve it. Change it. Make it funnier. If there isn't a big laugh at least every fifteen seconds, *put one in*. Then: Sleep On It. Go to bed and look at your material when you wake up in the morning. If it's still as funny as you thought it was when you wrote it, great! If it isn't, *throw it away*. Don't waste your time trying to rescue an idea that doesn't work. Go on to writing a *new* sketch. Be brutal with your own work. Only try and sell work you are totally happy with.

Hit Rate

For every good sketch you write, you should be throwing away about ten. Think of sketch writing as being a totally disposable art form. Don't be precious about your work. Comedy is as much about what you *don't* write as what you do write. But remember: Whatever you do, keep scribbling.

Get Clues

You must be persistent. If the editor or producer you're sending work to doesn't want to buy it, ask him or her why? If he doesn't want your type of material, what DOES he want? Ask him. Try and get a few clues as to what he finds funny: Does he like Jim Carey or John Cleese? In the long term, this will help you to write material that he *will* buy.

Unfortunately, rejection is part of the game. Be prepared to find out that some people do not have the same sense of humour as you have or don't roar with laughter at the things you write or say.

It doesn't matter if you're talking about death, religion, God, cancer; no matter how serious, solemn or tragic the question at hand, it can always be dealt with in a humorous fashion. This is not to say that to do so will always be socially appropriate, merely that the thing is possible.

Perseverance is the name of the game. Have faith in your own belief that you can do it.

Above all, keep writing!

Good Luck
Eddie